BE THE CHANGE

Transforming Health Care From the Inside Out

Jane L. Murray, MD

© 2011   Jane Murray
ISBN-10 1461157846
ISBN-13   978-1461157847

This book is dedicated to the many wonderful people from whom I have learned over the years – 'official' professors, my parents, many colleagues, mentors and friends, but most of all my patients, who continue to be my greatest source of inspiration, education and fulfillment.

This book is particularly dedicated to my big brother, Michael Murray, who passed away unexpectedly in 2010. My love and appreciation go to him wherever he is in the universe. We all will keep his memory very special in our hearts forever.

ACKNOWLEDGEMENTS

No book is written in a vacuum. So many people have helped me along this path from the birth of an idea to the printed page. Early in the process many friends and relatives read the first drafts and gave me good advice. For this I am deeply indebted to my brother Michael Murray, friends and mentors Walter Ricci, Victoria Moran, Davida Seliger, Linda Rostenberg. As the creative process dragged on and more (many more!) drafts were written, more friends and colleagues helped: Tammy Mikinski, Laura Mead, Connie Kerstetter, Betsy Holland, and my sister Diana Murray Smith.

Many kudos go to my tireless agents JoLynne Worley and Joanie Shoemaker for their innumerable hours spent trying to get publishers interested in this book. They helped me take the rejections in stride, and have facilitated immensely in this actual work seeing the light of day.

How could any book have a more beautiful cover than the art of fellow Kansan Jane Booth? She has been so excited and generous in helping set the tone of this story from the very first glance. And I am so honored to have art of her caliber grace this cover.

And finally, my greatest love and appreciation go to my husband Chris, who has cheered me on all these years and supported my many crazy ideas without missing a beat. He is my biggest fan and I know I can never thank him enough for his unconditional love and always present support.

Table of Contents

INTRODUCTION

The American health care system has been in crisis for decades. **No one has been happy** - not patients, not doctors, not insurance companies, not employers who must purchase insurance plans, not health administrators, not most other health professionals who work in the system, not government. All are disappointed and dissatisfied. As employers who select and pay for the chosen health plans, and as patients, we pay more every year and feel we receive less. As physicians and other "providers," we feel forced to give increasingly impersonal illness care, rather than real health care. As payers, we cannot seem to keep things under control as costs and expectations escalate. As a society, we have seen more and more of our citizens left out of the system entirely, as **over** 47 million Americans have lacked health insurance – most of these working families with children.

In 2010 we finally got concrete reform bills through Congress. All the reforms relate to improvements in the insurance system, payment mechanisms and potential upgrades in the overall structure of information exchange and communication among providers and payers. Not much is being done to transform the focus of care, the content of what will be delivered or many other priorities that need to be addressed. But it is a start. And it is fraught with controversy, anger and confusion. Change. Many will push back to try to repeal the new law, and how it will affect each of us over the next decade remains to be seen.

But while the pundits pontificate, the politicians debate, the protestors rally, the special interests dig in their heels, and the rest of us wait and wait to see what this "health care reform" is really about – something is happening. New approaches to prevention and healing are sowing the seeds of real reform – perhaps even transformation – of our health care system. Interventions involving acupuncture, herbal therapy, nutrition and mind-body medicine are having as important an impact on improving health and health care as new drugs and technology.

Everyone wants a quick fix for our delivery system. We'd like "them" (government, insurance companies, employers, hospitals, drug companies) to make changes that will benefit us as consumers. Many of us have felt as if we have been victims with little recourse except complaining, ever more loudly. "Someone should fix this terrible system," we shouted!! And yet, we patients have grudgingly gone along with selecting a new physician each year as our employer changed our health plan. We ask for pills for our ills instead of taking responsibility for our lifestyle choices. We physicians continue to go on working for the big health systems, hospitals and medical groups and collecting our paychecks, silently wondering, "Is that all there is?" in terms of personal and professional fulfillment. As employers, we struggle to offer our employees a good benefits package, but have to compromise our values about choice and autonomy, and sometimes even quality, to cut costs. Health executives spend much of their time wondering how to maintain quality while keeping costs at bay, rarely having time or courage to ask the fundamental questions about the ethics of the organizations for which they work. They collect their generous incomes while denying benefits to enrollees or, more impersonally, the company's "covered lives." Politicians, debate how and when to add prescription drug benefits for Medicare beneficiaries, instead of being honest about why identical drugs made by the same company cost so much more in the U.S. than elsewhere. They reduce costs in ever-shrinking budgets by limiting Medicaid coverage and cutting people off from needed benefits. Yet elected legislators keep their own generously funded health care plans for themselves, compliments of the U.S. taxpayers.

The truth is we all have to make our own health a high priority, and take responsibility for being as healthy as possible. Without good health, we cannot fully participate in life. We have to take responsibility for our lifestyle choices, for finding practitioners who will work with us to achieve and maintain good health and help us prevent disease and disability whenever possible.

When enough of us discover the value of optimum health for our families, our communities and ourselves the tipping point of demand for **health** care will overcome the current market for illness care. And integrative practitioners are there to deliver.

It now appears that reform is moving forward. Important changes in insurance regulation and ways for more Americans to have access may now be a reality. But we must also be aware that with this crucial legislation, it is not really someone else's responsibility to "fix the system" - each participant in the process needs to change his or her own expectations and change our own behavior. No system can change unless we each, and all, change. Are we up to this challenge?

This book is dedicated to the belief that we **can** decide to become different, and that we will always find a way to organize key aspects of our culture for true human benefit. This book is part memoir, part catharsis, and part vision quest for a better way. It is a personal journey born out of disappointment, frustration – even anger. It is a reflection of deep sadness that the long-honored profession of medicine is losing its luster, and practitioners and recipients of the art often feel that health care has misplaced not only its heart but also its soul. This book is also a rejection of the victim role we so often fall into when things aren't going right.

The chapters that follow are a quest for a healthy system, born from hope, optimism and a belief that humans can rise above discontentment, anger and blame to build a world that values the soul, caresses the heart, and nurtures the co-participants in this enterprise we call "health care."

And while no one was really looking or planning, legislating or pontificating, integrative medicine has started to creep onto the American health care scene. More and more people have decided to pay out of their own pockets for care not often covered by insurance: for acupuncture, massage, meditation classes, yoga, body work, lifestyle counseling, because they find these techniques work. The National Center for Health Statistics published that $34 billion was spent in 2007 (the latest year for which this data is available) on complementary and alternative therapies, and virtually none of that expense is reimbursed or covered by insurance. These expenditures account for 11.2% of all out of pocket health care dollars spent. Integrative medicine is becoming increasingly popular with the public, and more physicians are learning about how to incorporate it into their practices. This book also describes how integrative medicine may actually be the key to transforming American health care, from the inside out.

My Story

I've had a great education, both formally and in life experience. I graduated from the UCLA School of Medicine in 1977, having received my undergraduate degree from that institution in 1973. During college, I helped start a program whereby students were trained to serve their fellow students as peer health advisors in the dormitories, fraternities and sororities, the "Health Advocates" program, still going strong today.

As I went through medical school at UCLA I enjoyed every rotation. Learning was exciting, and the opportunity to try to help individuals coping with illness was thrilling. I decided family practice was the specialty area in which I could really develop relationships with people over time, and also use skills I was learning from all areas of medicine. I have been especially attracted to the emotional connections between illness and health. As teachers and upper classmates would ask my specialty choice, they would often recoil and ask "Why would a smart student like you want to be *just* a family physician?"

However, my family and friends would always be so pleased – "Oh, good! We need wonderful doctors to take care of us as whole people. Medicine has become so fragmented, we don't have anyone to call on when we need a doctor." These interchanges occurred over 30 years ago and they ring even more true today.

After medical school, I completed a three-year family practice residency in 1980 at Santa Monica Hospital. I loved my residency, except for the long hours and many nights on call, and the subsequent fatigue the next few days. My first professional position after residency training was teaching in that same residency in Southern California for six years. Our teaching practice was focused primarily on a medically underserved population, largely Spanish-speaking people. I also volunteered as a physician and served on the board of a local free clinic for many years.

For the next four and a half years I worked full time as Director of Education for the American Academy of Family Physicians, one of the largest medical specialty societies in the United States. My job involved a variety of diverse and exciting activities - much of my time devoted to health policy issues related to physician workforce and education. I also observed first-hand the many ways the pharmaceutical industry influences American medicine, especially in physicians' continuing education and medical research.

Next, I chaired a large department of family medicine at the University of Kansas School of Medicine in Kansas City for seven years. I experienced the difficult issues facing medical education and academic health centers today. I gained wide experience in developing new programs, managing people, teaching students and residents, and trying to work within a large bureaucracy at a tumultuous time in American health care.

I left academic medicine to open a practice of integrative medicine in 1998, which will be described in Chapter 2.   It has been a very liberating experience. I departed from the mainstream system of managed care and of business people running health care. I am proving that an alternative way to practice medicine is viable and very much appreciated by patients who are seeking a more caring, personal approach to their health and illness care. I am much happier and experiencing joy in my daily practice of medicine again. I have returned to the roots of why I wanted to be a physician in the first place.

"Change of Life" Creates a Life Change

It is no coincidence that this book with these concepts is written by a woman transitioning through midlife. This is a time when women often find their voice and are no longer afraid to speak.   I have had a lot of valuable and enlightening experiences in health care in the last thirty years, and it's time for me to speak out and share them. In fact, I started writing this book over ten years ago. I thought I held some very strong convictions about what "should" happen to fix our diseased system, and had the first several drafts of this book completed. Then, as it will, life happened.

I had more personal issues to cope with regarding the health care system and its many problems. My mother became very ill, and had a number of surgeries and hospitalizations. Shortly before she died in 2001, my husband was diagnosed with cancer, and more experiences as a patient and family member of a person dealing with the health care system again demanded a relocation of my perspective on how health care "should" change. Through the last several years my mother-in-law had multiple health challenges, surgeries and hospitalizations, and passed away in 2004. I discovered that I had to put writing this book on hold for a while, until I could really process all that happened to my loved ones and to me. I needed to reflect both on how deeply grateful I am for the wonders of modern medicine which have literally saved my husband's life, as well as for the difficulties we have subsequently had to face regarding insurance, health care costs, and non-insurability. With both of our mothers, we encountered many incredibly wonderful, caring and competent health care professionals, and some not so caring, some with no ability to communicate, and occasionally ones who committed significant medical errors.

All these life events are the same things that happen to all of us. We, or our loved ones, need services for serious or life-threatening problems. We are grateful we live in a country that has made such profound medical advances as bone marrow transplantation for cancer and surgery to repair a fractured neck become daily occurrences. Yet many Americans – especially those on fixed incomes - live in constant fear of being unable to afford medications, the next insurance premium hike or the health care crisis that could literally bankrupt us.

My purpose in writing this book is to try to put into words what so many Americans, from all walks of life, are experiencing as a health care system with many failings; what too many physicians, in all specialties, are sensing as an erosion of the joy and honor of practicing medicine in today's environment; what so many employers are struggling with in trying to provide proper benefits to their employees at a cost that is affordable. I am a participant in all of these groups, coping with all of these perspectives that say we need a change. And as a patient, family member, physician and employer, I realize that we all will have to change if we want our system to serve us better. I also see that my experiences with integrative medicine both as a practitioner and recipient give me hope for a transformed system, even if we do not get all the legislated system changes that might be possible, or if they are demolished by special interests.

Hope as Motivator

Thus, this book is written in the hope that the spark of transformation might be kindled within others who participate in health care in various capacities and roles: people who are feeling unsettled, unhappy, perhaps actually angry by the role they are filling and the contribution they are personally making to our problematic system by continuing to buy into it. A system cannot change unless and until its constituents begin to change. When we each become different – make different decisions based on our core values, and then have the courage to change our behavior – other components will have to change in order to interface with us. We can improve and "fix" health care, but not through coercion or force, and not entirely by legislation. We can change the system by changing ourselves - one at a time.

Let's take a lesson from the history of independence in India. Mahatma Gandhi, the remarkable leader of a peaceful revolution, defeated the entire British colonial government. He accomplished this feat not through coercion or armed conflict, but through the powerful, quiet spiritual commitment of one gentle man. His actions took on their own life, and gathered support from millions of people in India. He believed that peaceful protest based on personal values and priorities could change nations. He was right. Gandhi said, "*You must be the change you wish to see in the world.*"

Are we ready to <u>be</u> that change?

CHAPTER 1

WALKING OFF A CLIFF

Eleven months into my new job as chair of a medical school clinical department, I had a chilling revelation. My values and priorities were in startling conflict with those of some of my superiors. A few individuals in leadership positions at that time seemed to me not to really understand the mission of a great university and publicly funded medical center. Their behavior indicated that they were there for reasons of their own importance, not for service. (*And I should quickly point out at this juncture that nearly all the people in leadership positions at the institution are new since my departure, and reports of their leadership abilities have been very positive.*)

This awareness made me question my idealism about public service, teaching, and the ongoing quest for progress through research and education. I believed that enough good people working hard enough could eventually overcome a lack of leadership vision and vigor. I was wrong – leadership is everything. The values and beliefs of the leader create the organizational environment.

I had read Sally Helgeson's 1992 book *Female Advantage: Women's Ways of Leadership,* and felt strongly that women's wisdom about "webs of inclusion" and good communication in the workplace could transform organizations.

Human groups based on relationship networks that allow people to communicate and interface effectively are proving to be more successful than those based on hierarchical structures with rigid rules for interaction. I had written an editorial titled "Women Leaders Rock the Boat" for a family practice magazine. In it, I predicted that it would be women leaders in medicine who would be largely responsible for needed change in health care and in medical education, because women, in general, are more experienced with relationship building and communication that is inclusive rather than hierarchical. I really believed if I worked hard enough, I could impact those needed changes in my institution, and create what Helgesen calls "webs of inclusion."

I plugged away for six more years, through numerous new administrators, and new structures, each time hoping the new leader would bring a courage of values and a true caring for the people involved at least as much as the process. But, from my perspective, nothing substantially changed. I held on to the hope for change because I knew about "transformational leadership." I had worked in organizations previously with this type of leadership, and knew firsthand it was definitely possible.

My job immediately preceding academia was working within a large medical membership organization, the American Academy of Family Physicians. The AAFP's CEO, Robert Graham, MD, was not only a visionary, but a wonderful manager as well. He was incredibly intelligent, and also had the "emotional intelligence" to understand his employees, colleagues and constituents and how to work effectively with people. I always knew he was telling the truth. He respected other people's opinions and strengths. He was a model for me of a leader who set the tone, ethics and integrity for everyone else in the organization, and it worked very well.

Prior to the Academy job, I had worked as a faculty member in a residency program in a large community hospital. Our director was another visionary physician – Sanford Bloom, MD – who exhibited honesty and integrity and commitment to patient care and resident education. He was a superb role model for so many future doctors. He spent time and energy nurturing us to be good physicians, and to take on responsibility for administrative and leadership positions also. He gave me more "opportunities for growth" than I felt I could handle at times, but was a mentor in every sense of that word. He helped his people develop. He did not just use them to get a particular job done.

Having had these two previous experiences in organizations that functioned well - largely due to the character of their leaders - I was terribly disappointed with my situation. Disillusionment, however, may be a prerequisite for growth and change, so I could consider this career episode in medical academia a major "growth experience."

I came into academic management **not** from prior research or academic experience, but from organizational medicine. At the time, the department was in some need of management skills, and that is what I brought. I felt I accomplished a great deal in the seven years I chaired the department. We began a rather vigorous research program with federal grants and several new faculty members dedicated to research (this is very important in a medical school department.) We created some new training opportunities for our residents in rural communities – again quite important for a rural state like Kansas to prepare doctors for their ultimate practice. We were successful in increasing medical student interest in becoming family doctors, and improved the quality of our residency. We were able to expand our faculty, and had significant impact upon curriculum reform in the medical school, with the infusion of significant grant money from the Kansas Health Foundation. We helped nurture a fledgling telemedicine program into an important part of the university's role in providing specialty care to remote areas of our state. I was proud of these accomplishments and had a lot of help from many outstanding people to see these programs flourish.

Toward the end of my term as chair, I received an excellent review by a committee appointed by the Dean. The one area of weakness in my leadership was that the department was struggling financially, as was every other department in our school and almost all other medical schools in the country at that time.

But the satisfaction of my self-perceived successes was badly marred by my self-perceived lack of support for my department by others in the institution, and by lack of commitment to important principles I saw around me on a daily basis. Episodes like the attending surgeon who never actually examined my patient after surgery and that the only progress notes in the chart for several days running were by a medical student, caused me ethical concerns. This event was not isolated, and occurred during a time in medicine (the mid-1990's) when the federal government was investigating medical schools for just this type of legal infraction; the surgeon seemed oblivious that this behavior on his part was a problem.

Or episodes like the university physicians' practice group purchasing a health plan for our employees that did not include our group as participating physicians. When a few of us protested that this might be sending our employees a negative message, we were admonished that, as a practice group, we were "running a business and have to be concerned about the bottom line, not about messages."

Or like total disregard by other chairs and the group practice managers for facts that were in black and white for all to see about our family medicine department's superior performance in hospital length of stay and cost per discharge compared to other departments; or the fact that we had the highest number of dollars of federal research money per faculty member of any department in the institution at that time. Or the fact that after developing and nurturing a home for telemedicine, which might have eventually brought some prestige and research funding for our department, telemedicine was unceremoniously moved to another administrative area in the medical center via a phone call one day while I was seeing patients in the clinic, no face-to-face meeting or discussion was held. These rather major frustrations along with other daily minor irritations began to add up.

Physical Pain as a Warning Sign

It was my body that finally forced me to take a realistic look at the situation. After a particularly 'difficult day at the office' – one in which my department's state-legislated funding was threatened to be removed – I developed chest pain and a cardiac arrhythmia.

Never before had a serious, life-threatening health problem in my own body stared me in the face. I called my family doctor, and was directed immediately to the University's emergency room. I felt confident in my doctors, from ER to family physicians to cardiologists. The nurses were wonderful. I wasn't exactly scared, but I knew this was a wake up call. Even while still in the hospital lying flat with my leg immobilized after the coronary angiogram, I knew I had to quit. The job was not right for me, nor I for it. I had to disentangle myself from what I experienced as a poorly functioning (i.e. "dysfunctional") organization, and realize that my vision for an effective organizational structure was in conflict with the current reality.

In truth, most of the families we come from could be considered "dysfunctional." No parent is perfect, and all of us are born with or develop at least some human frailties, neuroses, and emotional scars. Then we bring these into our workplace, and often find ourselves in organizations and institutions that mirror the problems in relationships with which we became familiar growing up. It is no wonder that most organizations could probably be described as dysfunctional. They are led by and composed of people with human frailties, neuroses and emotional scars. But the current organizational family I was in seemed to me to have just _too_ many problems. Key individuals in leadership positions did not even speak to one another much less cooperate or collaborate. The governing board of the physicians' practice plan consisted of a cumbersome group of over 30 individuals with very diverse agendas - all attempting to organize a complex medical group. No one was actually in charge of anything, and so no one really made any meaningful decisions and progress was virtually impossible. After years of trying to provide leadership, I realized I had failed, and I felt I had to give up.

I had never actually quit anything before. I had moved on, of course, always with a clear destination already lined up. But quitting because it did not feel right, with no planned "next step" was foreign. However, I decided this job, this chairmanship, was not worth dying for. I pictured in my mind the conference room where the department chairs met every two weeks with the Dean, at five p.m. on Thursdays. I mentally scanned the table, picturing the faces of the 18 men and 2 women. Three had already had coronary artery bypass surgery to repair a blocked blood supply to the heart. One was being treated for cancer. Two retired chairs had survived earlier heart attacks. Is this what I wanted for myself? No way, I decided.

Fortunately my coronary angiogram – the x-ray study done to see whether the heart arteries are blocked - was perfectly clear. It's reassuring to know at age 46 your heart is healthy! Now for the real question, the difficult one: am I strong enough to make the decision to transform my life?

Become the Change

What I knew I had to do was change **me**.   I had to
realize that my actual abilities did not include changing the world.
I had to admit that I could not change a university medical
center, or even significantly change a department that had to
exist within that medical center. I needed to see if I could
actually practice medicine again; on my own, in a way that not
only valued and served patients properly, but also valued and
nurtured my self.

I had always felt uncomfortable with being the
intermediary between the patient and the payer. 'Managed care,'
while an intriguing concept with much to commend it in theory,
was turning out to be a nightmare in many ways for 'providers'
(i.e. doctors and hospitals) as well as for patients. Why did we
physicians agree to become the go-between? Why were we
accepting payment from the payer and providing the service to
the patient, buffering a nearly complete disconnection between
the recipient of the service (i.e. the patient) and the payment
source (i.e. the insurance company?) When did we agree to
become "providers?" And when did we start accepting
descriptive terms for our patients such as "beneficiary,"
"recipient," "insured," or "covered life," and even start using
these terms ourselves?

I had also always wondered if it would be possible, as a
primary care physician, to be paid for my time – so much per
minute or hour like psychotherapists or plumbers or mechanics –

rather than by diagnosis or procedure as is the current way to pay doctors. The thought seemed reasonable to me.

Integrating Complementary Therapies

I also decided that any healing method that could help a person and not be harmful was something I could openly accept. I had long been a closet 'holistic' physician, occasionally using hands-on healing with patients and referring people to chiropractors and acupuncturists. I discussed with patients blocked chakra energy and its relationship to physical symptoms. I used mind-body practices in the exam room: progressive muscle relaxation, guided imagery and relaxation breathing. I was always discussing stress with people, and looking at ways they could work on managing it more effectively. Many of these practices are natural for family physicians – we want to do whatever we can to help patients find the tools to heal, and many of us have been trained in some or all of these techniques.

Over time, I developed relationships in the community with a variety of healing professionals – chiropractors, massage therapists, an acupuncturist – and had ongoing discussions about how great it would be to incorporate these modalities together in the same physical space to help patients. We did have a nurse practitioner in our department who decided to seek training in massage therapy. When she finished the program, we set up a small room for her to provide massage in our clinic on a limited basis. This was a very novel idea in the mid 1990's in Kansas.

I really wanted to bring acupuncture and other complementary therapies into our clinic, but I had felt some of my views were not really acceptable in a large medical center environment, so kept it quiet at the time. Today, of course, many medical centers are scrambling to figure out how to offer "holistic" or "complementary" or "integrative" health services. Too often, they are organizing such clinics along the same biomedical model that is now failing us. Sometimes these services are seen by the organization as just a way to bring in "market share," not to substantially change the terrain of health care delivery. More on this subject is found in Chapter 4.

Serious Change is in Order

So, what I did was walk off a cliff. I wanted to open a practice where I would not participate in any HMO panels or PPO lists. I would actually charge people for my time, and give them enough time to tell their story and be fully heard. I decided to practice with a small group of non-physician colleagues in the community: a practitioner of Oriental Medicine – herbs and acupuncture, a counselor and a craniosacral therapist, people I had been communicating with about this idea over time. I took out a business loan at a local bank. We found office space we liked and could afford. We developed a modest business plan.

I arranged to continue teaching part time at the medical school, and helped develop a curriculum in complementary medicine. I had written a successful grant related to community medicine during my tenure as department chair, and agreed to continue working on its implementation. Fortunately, this gave me a small but predictable income, and I very much appreciated this arrangement.

Unfortunately, I lost all the benefits I had previously enjoyed – health insurance, life and disability insurance, paid memberships in professional organizations, paid vacation and sick leave, paid continuing education time, and an excellent pension plan. I lost my built-in practice coverage as well. For the first time in my life, I was not someone else's full time employee. I was on my own.

Many of my friends and colleagues applauded my courage; some thought I was nuts. Personally, I was scared to death. But I kept envisioning the scene in the movie *Indiana Jones and the Last Crusade* in which Harrison Ford is instructed to "take a leap of faith," sure to fall to his death in the infinite abyss in his search for the Holy Grail. He doesn't want to do it. He is really scared. But the message insists: "Take a leap of faith." And as he does – a bridge instantly forms under his feet. In fact the bridge was there all the time, he just couldn't see it. Quite a metaphor for us in our daily lives!

Somewhere, just beyond concrete reality, I actually believed such a bridge would form for me, too, and that I would not fall into a bottomless canyon of failure and financial ruin. I kept this vision of Indiana Jones in my mind – to use whenever I got too scared.

I learned several valuable lessons in this process. One was that I had been living much of my life on the basis of fear:

"What happens if I don't have enough money?" "What happens if I get sick and have to take off work – then there's no income coming in, but overhead continues?" "Will I ever be able to afford a vacation again?" All the questions every self-employed person has had to face. Another fear was that inner scare of self-sufficiency: Can I really support myself without the safety net of the big organization? Even more worrisome: "What if no patients come? Maybe they'll only show up if I am on their insurance plan's list of participating doctors." "Will they really pay me for my services?"

Then, of course, there is the fear of practicing a bit differently from others. Most doctors are quite conservative, and do not want to practice "outside the mainstream." We are afraid of malpractice suits, of our license being taken away, of Medicare and insurance audits, of censure by our colleagues. In some ways we are trained to be lemmings, not forward thinkers. So much of our practice life is based on fear. But how can we ever make progress if we do not venture past our comfortable boundaries?

Paradigm Pioneering

A friendly colleague told me early on in my decision-making process that there are three kinds of people: "paradigm shifters," "paradigm pioneers" and "paradigm settlers." 'Paradigm shifters' are those few people who can see the future and see a better way, and bring others to the view that a social structure can, should and will change. The next group, the 'pioneers', are the first people "out of the box". They are the scouts who go forth and see how the new model could work, with no roadmap or clear direction. They are risk takers, adventurers perhaps. The third group, the 'settlers' are the ones who hold back, live life in the mainstream and periodically ask the pioneers "Is it safe yet?" Only when the new terrain has been tested, accurate maps delineated and the new paradigm made safe, will the settlers start to arrive. My friend told me I was a "paradigm pioneer" forging into the unknown world of integrative medicine and not participating in insurance plans. I liked that role. I usually am not the one to give birth to fabulous new ideas or blueprints, but I am willing to take the risk to try out new formats that may be better than the ones we've got. Very few people are the shifters; a few more are the pioneers; most are settlers.

Second, I learned there is a big price to pay for the security provided by a regular paycheck and benefits. You have to live by that Golden Rule – "He who has the gold, rules." Whoever holds the purse strings calls the shots. Even as a medical school department chair with a certain amount of autonomy, I discovered health care has become an extremely difficult system to operate, with virtually no autonomy. The payers call the shots. The administrators call the shots. The doctors rarely do, and even less frequently do the patients have a say. In the academic setting, there is less freedom every year; more control by the "marketplace," and by the fiscal administrators. The ability to really do what one believes is right in the right way is constantly overridden by cost constraints, administrators insisting more patients be seen with less support staff, in less time, using fewer resources.

The third lesson I learned was that straying from the mainstream, if liberating, can be lonely. Having colleagues with whom to share cases, get a "curbside" consult and commiserate is very valuable. Doing something a different way puts one outside the circle, and isolation can be tough.

Finally, I learned what I already really knew: we all have choices. Sometimes it feels as if we don't. We doctors think we have to be on at least some insurance plans, if not many. We have to have some secure income. We have to practice a certain way or we'll be targets for malpractice litigation, fraud investigation, licensing censure or criticism from our peers. We often act as if we are victims of a terrible system and have no choices. We forget that we can choose what we believe is best for us and for our patients, and which potential consequences we are willing to accept. In fact, we really have to realize that we are responsible for every choice we make at every step in our lives. What we usually want, my psychologist friend told me, are "pain free" choices. Unfortunately, those are few and far between in life.

I had a pivotal experience shortly before I decided what I would do after resigning from the chair position, which clarified for me this issue of choices and consequences.

A Life-Changing Revelation

I was paged about 11:30 one night from an emergency room in our community. The nurse stated that one of my patients was there after having had a seizure. This patient was a person I had never met and did not know, but my name was on her insurance card as her primary care physician. This is a common practice for managed care plans – patients select a doctor from a booklet given to them by the benefits manager at work. This doctor is the "PCP," or primary care physician who must authorize all tests, treatments, hospital admissions, referrals to specialists, etc. Usually the patient and physician have no pre-existing relationship; many times they do not even meet.

At any rate, the emergency department physician got on the phone and wanted me to approve this woman's admission to his hospital, even though it was an "out of network" facility for her health plan. I asked if he felt she could be safely transferred to an in-network hospital. He said no. I said, "Well, of course, then, admit her there."

I was angry. Why was I being called late at night about a patient I did not know, in order to approve something that was obviously necessary? I was mad at the health plan. I was mad at the ER doctor. I was mad at the unknown patient. Then I realized something crucially important: I had agreed to be part of a large multispecialty group practice that had contracts with health plans that operated in this way. So I couldn't really be mad at anybody. I could only be mad at my decision to participate in such craziness. If I didn't want to be held accountable for patients I didn't even know, then I needed to decide not to participate in such plans. I decided that night not to be a member of a group that signed contracts with managed care plans. I decided I needed to try practicing medicine my own way.

As the Zen masters would say, I needed to find my "right livelihood."

CHAPTER 2

CONFRONTING A SYSTEM OUT OF CONTROL

Ten months after my cardiac scare, I opened an integrative health care practice with three non-physician colleagues: a practitioner of Oriental Medicine, a counselor and a craniosacral therapist (see **Glossary** for the definition of terms that may be unfamiliar.) The three of them already had thriving practices; I was the one who had to build a patient base. We met frequently over several months to plan our new arrangement, find space, and begin a new model of practice. We call our practice the Sastun Center of Integrative Health Care.

The word "sastun" is what traditional Mayan healers call their personal healing amulet. It can be a stone, a crystal or some other found object and these healers believe the sastun gives them their healing power. The word actually derives from "sas-" meaning light and "-tun" meaning stone or age in the Mayan language. So "sastun" literally means "light of the ages" and symbolizes the deep roots of tradition of various therapeutic practices as well as the healing essence within each person. We explain that the path to an individual's personal healing may be different one from another, and that many healing options may be helpful as they seek their own optimal health, their own "sastun."

My resolve to not participate in health plans meant that patients would pay me at the time of service and then submit paperwork themselves to the insurance company for reimbursement. We supply the proper forms with all the necessary codes and information, and the patient sends that in to his or her insurance company with a claim form. Unless the patient is in a capitated HMO plan which was already paying a designated physician or group a monthly fee for the person's health care, the person usually receives 50-80% reimbursement for my care as an "out of network provider," but some get even less, or nothing back, depending upon the particular insurance plan's rules. Some people have no insurance or a high deductible plan anyway, so seeing me is no different for them than seeing any doctor.

The first year I saw a slowly increasing number of patients. People came as a result of an article our local newspaper printed about our new kind of practice. A local television station did a nice profile on our unique center. Chiropractors and other "alternative" practitioners referred people to a doctor who might be open minded about health care options. But mostly, as with any new business, the practice grew by word-of-mouth. There were weeks when I thought I was crazy. No one showed up. New patients cancelled their appointments, or just didn't come. There were very few appointments on the schedule, anyway. I took home no paycheck from the practice the first year. Thank goodness for a very supportive husband, savings, my part-time job at the medical school, and some kind of blind faith that it would all "work out."

My relationship with money definitely changed. For years I had been very financially comfortable. I had a newly remodeled house, a good car, the ability to travel the world, eat out any time, and buy clothes and gifts at will. If I wanted something, I pretty much bought it. I've never had extravagant taste, but shopping has always been a fun pastime.

Suddenly, I had to decide if I really needed new clothes, or new shoes. Could we really afford raspberries and asparagus this week? Which restaurant did we have a coupon for? I kind of went into culture shock. I had to live much more frugally – the way most Americans do. I realized I had plenty of clothes – too many, really. I like to cook, and it's a lot cheaper to eat at home. Not traveling was probably the most difficult for us, but we enjoyed our yard and going to movies more. I actually feel lucky to have had the chance to re-evaluate the purpose of money and my relationship to it.

While reflecting on money, I have to admit another conflict arose for me in what could be called my "soul quest." My entire professional career has had a component of service to the underserved. My residency, then first practice and teaching position was with a largely underserved population. I sat on the boards of directors of two free clinics over many years. I have always donated time to charity care. Now I am in this practice where I charge cash for my services, and have fees that will actually cover my costs. How do I reconcile these commitments to caring for those in need, while experimenting with a new model that requires immediate payment? One personal consolation is that I do see some patients at no charge. We work out payment plans for those in need. I make markedly less money than I have in any of my previous salaried positions, so I have to be careful about how much free care I can provide. In the past, I could afford to provide charity care – I was making a good living through some large organization's ability to carry the charity burden.

I also have rationalized that I am experimenting with a new model of practice. As we prove what can work and what cannot in integrative care, and we all learn more about what is effective and what is not, all the services that are beneficial should become available to everyone in some way. When we have a medical system that enfranchises everyone, then all of us will equally share the "burden" of charity care. But I am still very concerned about universal access to care, so more on this topic in Chapter 3.

Confronting the Costs of Health Care

I learned some important lessons about people and money by setting up my practice in the unconventional way I did. Patients actually see their bill. They see what each service and lab test costs, and how much they are paying for my time with them. They have to decide if this cost is worthwhile. Even if they eventually get much of their payment to me reimbursed by their insurance, a connection is made between service and money. I have had many more "cost effectiveness" discussions with my patients in this practice than in previous situations. When people assume "my insurance (or Medicare/Medicaid) is paying for all this" they really do not have to consider the cost-benefit issues. I have this same conversation with innumerable friends and patients. They mention that as soon as their annual deductible is paid, they want all the tests they think might be interesting to have, since "it doesn't cost me anything now."

There is something about the process of facing the actual bill and understanding the cost of a CT scan or MRI, a blood test or a half hour of discussion with the doctor that brings into focus for the patient whether that information or service is really of value to them. Even if the cost is reimbursed, it is important for people to have some concept of the real costs of tests, treatments, and the doctor's time – above and beyond their deductible and co-pays.

Our payment system today has generally created a complete "disconnect" for people between services and costs. Patients often feel the **only** cost of health care is their office co-pay and annual deductible. They are insulated from the true cost of care by itemized bills going from the doctor or hospital to the insurance company directly and completely bypassing the patient. Even if insurance is going to pay for the services, the importance of a personal investment in the process is lost. And perhaps the cost of health care is being escalated because there is no consumer input in our current system.   An interesting example of this cost inflation occurred to me when I was a patient several years ago.

A Personal Story

I needed to have an invasive radiology procedure done in a hospital requiring a one-night stay, the use of the radiology suite and a few medications. I was having excessively heavy menstrual periods due to a benign fibroid tumor in my uterus. The size and position of this fibroid was perfect for an arterial embolization procedure, whereby the radiologist visualizes the uterine arteries with dye, then injects a material which blocks the blood supply to the offending fibroid, and essentially "kills" it. This wonderful procedure saved me a hysterectomy. I was becoming very anemic and easily fatigued with the blood loss caused by these heavy periods. I needed to do something. Being now self-employed, with no covered sick time, I could not afford to take four to six weeks off work to recover from major surgery. So the embolization was the perfect option for me.

At first, my insurance company (through my husband's employer at the time) was not sure they would cover this service, and I received a bill from the hospital for over $29,000. I was shocked. I could not imagine what sort of open-heart operation or brain surgery the hospital must have charged for. I was sure there was some kind of mistake. My comparison was a bill my mother-in-law received at about the same time for a complicated orthopedic neck surgery, including three days in the hospital, the use of the operating room, and rehabilitation services. Her total hospital bill for nearly three times more services than I received was only a little more than $15,000. Even though these hospitalizations occurred in different geographic regions of the country, this huge discrepancy seemed completely inappropriate.

I called the hospital I had been in for the overnight stay to get an itemized bill and verification that this was actually a bill for my hospitalization, and not some other patient. They insisted this was for me, and that these charges were correct. They promised to send me an itemized bill. While waiting several weeks to receive the itemization, I received correspondence from my insurance company stating that they had now decided to cover this procedure. The papers they sent showed that the hospital had charged them over $53,000. The insurance company paid them just over $23,000. Now I really wanted to see the bill the hospital submitted to the insurance company and find out why it was nearly twice the amount they had originally billed me. Something seemed very fishy, indeed.

The real clincher in this scenario, the one that makes me angry about the greed and insanity sometimes so pervasive in our system, is this: the day before my procedure was scheduled, a billing person from the radiologist's office had spoken to me about the possibility that the procedure would not be covered by insurance. If that were the case, the radiologist was offering me a discounted fee for a cash payment, and the hospital had agreed to accept $4,000 in cash from me as payment in full for the hospital bill.

So now I was very confused and frustrated by our system. I was happy to be spared the cost of the procedure (less deductibles and co-pays, of course!), and should have been grateful that the hospital would discount their bill to me so dramatically. But how can a hospital justify charging $53,000 to an insurance company for a procedure they had determined was actually worth $4,000 if paid for in cash? Where did the $29,000 original bill to me come from? And why would an insurance company pay $23,000 without any type of investigation?   Do you ever wonder why the cost of health care keeps skyrocketing? The price charged for services is very arbitrary, oftentimes not based on anything related to the actual costs incurred by the hospital to provide the service. It has been said "When individuals are insulated from the costs of decisions, there exists an inescapable formula for inflation." I think this is partly what is happening in our health care system today.

I did speak to the chief financial officer of the hospital about this bizarre situation. He was at a loss to explain why I received the original bill for $29,000. He said I should have been billed the full $53,000. He also claimed no knowledge of the earlier $4,000 "cash price" arrangement. He then went on to explain that the payers in California (this hospital is part of a rather notorious for-profit hospital chain in that state) are terribly low in what they pay. The hospital therefore has to charge high prices, because they know they will receive only a fraction of the billed charge. Does this really make any sense? Inflate your prices exorbitantly so you might get paid a fraction of them and possibly cover your actual costs? This is the pricing game being played around the country every day.

One example of this hospital's obscenely high prices included a $130 charge for a one-liter bag of intravenous fluid. I pay less than $3 for this same item in my office. They charged me for several medications I never received, such as insulin (for diabetes, which I fortunately do not have) and intravenous nitroglycerine (usually used for chest pain or other cardiac conditions, which I also do not have.) These drugs were also priced on my bill at hugely inflated fees, but were reversed when brought to the hospital's attention as errors. These sorts of erroneous charges are commonplace in hospitals around the country, but few patients ever see their bill, or if they do, are not necessarily knowledgeable enough to realize if the drugs and procedures billed for were actually administered, and whether the listed prices are reasonable or not.

More Erroneous and Exorbitant Charges

A patient named Tina related to me a similar story about her 82 year-old father's hospital experience when he had a stroke. Not only did she have to be an active advocate to see that he got the nursing care he needed, but also she reviewed his bill and found $5,400 of errors there. Tina realized it was very fortunate that she was able to participate in this situation, as her 80 year-old mother was in no condition to confront these issues, especially at a time she when was worrying about her spouse's health problems. Tina wondered what elderly or seriously ill people do when they don't have a family member such as her to help out in these situations. I wonder too.

Another patient, Joe, related the story of his son's birth several years ago. Because of some complications with the baby's initial breathing efforts, emergency activities were undertaken. Joe's son and wife were fine, but the family eventually received a $20,000 bill from the hospital. When Joe went over the bill in detail with the doctor, hundreds of dollars of items that were not used or procedures that were not performed were crossed off the bill. One wonders if hospitals just list a lot of extraneous items hoping no one will check and they will get paid more.

Why don't hospitals and doctors set their charges at rates that are reasonable, and then stick to those rates? We keep accepting discounts from Medicare and managed care organizations in order to keep a flow of patients, and then have to charge other patients exorbitant fees to make up the difference. Why shouldn't all payers – including Medicare and Medicaid - pay what the service is actually worth, not more, and not less?

I actually wrote a letter to my insurance company (after several unsuccessful attempts at calling them on the phone) to bring to their attention the fact that they had paid too much for my fibroid embolization. I never received any type of response from them. Maybe they are embarrassed at being gouged. Maybe they never received my letter. Maybe they have no protocol for a patient complaining that the charges were too high and that the company paid too much. I guess I'll never know.

Mary Jane, another patient shared an interesting "overcharging" story with me: she had gone to the hospital while living in South Dakota a few years ago for symptoms that were worrisome. She later received an EOB ("Explanation of Benefits") letter from her insurance company indicating that they had been billed $9,000 for a lab test, and paid it. Mary Jane thought that seemed like a very high charge for a lab test, and called the hospital's billing department to inquire about it. The clerk checked and told her the test was actually $900 and that someone must have accidentally entered an extra zero. So then Mary Jane called her insurance company who was very happy she had found the $8,100 error, but was unable to explain why they had not questioned this obviously incorrect charge and just paid it. Apparently the insurance company got their $8,100 refunded eventually, after several more phone calls by Mary Jane to the hospital and the insurance company. Her summary of this experience: "Is it any wonder why our health care and insurance costs are where they are today?"

An Exercise in Cost Comparison

A year after my California hospital extravaganza, my mother was hospitalized for 60 days in a university hospital not 5 miles from the for-profit unit I stayed at. She spent half of those two months in the intensive care unit, so her use of medical services was quite expensive. Remember my bill for the one night, low-risk stay was $53,000? Her hospital bill for 60 days, one month of that time in intensive care, was about $150,000, or three times the charge for much more than 60 times the care. And because she was a Medicare recipient, the hospital did not even receive their full charges. These non-profit, university and public hospitals are suffering severely with regard to financial viability. No wonder they struggle so hard to stay afloat financially, they never get paid what they charge, and nowhere near what they are worth.

So What **is** the Cost of Health Care?

Our system is out of control. We are losing confidence and trust in our hospitals and doctors when situations such as this occur. And they do occur – every day in every community in America. How do we know what the right "price" for a service actually is? How much does a given health service actually cost? What is the fee schedule for various procedures and services? More often than not, no one can tell us.

How can we compare prices for services if we are not told about them up front? It is very common, when calling a hospital to find out the cost of a chest x-ray or mammogram, for example, that no one there can actually quote a price. The price depends on what type of insurance you have, and what rate has been negotiated between your insurance company and the facility. Oftentimes there is no such thing as a "fee schedule." And because so many insurance companies have negotiated prices they will pay that are actually below the cost of the procedure, the facility or medical group charges the patients who have either no insurance or a better type of insurance a much higher fee to make up for the loss.

I have had many patients over the years who have only a catastrophic health insurance plan, with no coverage for routine care, preventive services, prescription coverage, etc., so they pay these costs out of their own pocket. This happened to a friend of mine, Liz, at a local university hospital. She had high deductible, catastrophic insurance and needed an expensive outpatient test. She asked the hospital billing department if they would give her the same discounted rate as they would give a patient's insurance company, but she would pay in cash and they would save the cost of billing and collecting. They said no, they couldn't give any discounts off their fees unless it had been negotiated with an insurance company. And remember, fees are almost always set at excessively high rates, because hospitals expect to be paid at a discount. So the person paying cash, like Liz, often ends up paying a lot more for a test or procedure than the insurance company of someone else receiving the same service or test. Insane? Unfair? Definitely.

When we as patients are completely outside the billing and communication loop, how do we know that our insurance company is not getting gouged? If I had not asked for an itemized bill, I would not have found the medication errors, nor seen the outrageous amounts being charged for each item and service. Why is there a greater than 10-fold disparity between costs billed to insurance and those that might have been accepted if paid upfront in cash, as happened in my case?

The answer is that there is no sense in the system. The payers decide what they will pay, and the doctors and hospitals roll over and play dead, accepting these lower fees and then complaining loudly about how unfair it all is. Maybe the providers (doctors and hospitals) could consider setting fees that are actually reasonable to cover their costs, and then not agree to accept lower fees. This idea seems to be such a radical concept in today's system, and yet it may be one of the simple changes that saves us. If all the providers behaved in this way, and made individual decisions, one by one, not to accept discounted fees, the payers would have to come up with a way to pay properly. What happens now is that doctors and hospitals are afraid if they don't negotiate lower fees they will be "shut out" of a certain insurance plan, and won't have any patients. Again, it seems we all work from a basic platform of fear. Rather than valuing what we are actually worth, and then sticking to our guns about how we will practice, we willingly subject ourselves to this institutionalized form of blackmail from insurance companies. And then we feel abused.

Government programs also need to pay the real price for the service. Medicare and especially Medicaid notoriously pay inadequate rates to cover the true costs of service. Until recent years, these programs as well as physicians and hospitals depended upon other patients with better coverage to make up the difference, and no one was too unhappy. Now, however, many managed care plans have negotiated fees even lower than Medicare payment, and the new economic survival technique for medical groups is to see more patients in the same amount of time, and make up in volume what they are losing in reimbursement. A troubling trend in recent years is the annual decrease in the Medicare fee schedule, so that doctors are actually being paid less each year for caring for Medicare patients. My usual fee for a 10-15 minute return visit is $70. Medicare paid $39.40 for this service in 2005. In 2006 this rate was reduced to $37.40. It is very difficult to cover overhead (which is typically in the 60-70% range for a primary care practice) when one of the major payers – Medicare – does not even cover basic overhead costs, much less any margin for the physician. I am happy to donate some of my own services to patients in need, but my landlord does not discount my rent, nor the phone company my phone bills, nor my office staff their salaries. I have to pay my bills, as does every other doctor, and the terribly low rates Medicare reimburses puts many doctors in a position to limit the number of Medicare patients they can afford to see, or discontinue accepting Medicare as a payer at all. This is what I finally decided to do in 2008 because I felt that a high volume practice where I would see 40-60 patients a day is NOT how I wish to spend my life. Unfortunately for many Medicare beneficiaries, more and more doctors are making this decision to "opt out" of Medicare.

Trying to compensate in volume what one loses in revenue per case eventually reaches the untenable point where one finally loses money on each patient seen in the office or cared for in the hospital. This scenario seems to be what is happening in California: the rates paid for services are so low, that anyone with an insurance that actually pays well appears to be being gouged. It's really a no-win situation for anyone, and must change.

Learned Helplessness

Another lesson I learned in setting up my new practice was the helplessness our current system promotes among many patients. When people call my office for an appointment as a new patient, we explain our policies regarding payment at the time of service and the patient's responsibility to submit to their insurance company the paperwork that we give them for reimbursement. Some are shocked that they must submit paperwork themselves. When we explain the simplicity of stapling our printed forms containing all the needed code numbers to one of their company's claim forms, some still ask, "Why can't you do that?" If a person cannot fathom stapling two pieces of paper together, folding them, putting them in an envelope with a stamp and mailing that envelope, I wonder how they are able to take responsibility every day for their health decisions. Will they feel responsible to eat properly, exercise, take medications properly, and get enough sleep? Or is all that activity someone else's job too?

We seem to have created a populace of disempowered individuals who frequently feel that it is the doctor's job to not only give them health but also to negotiate with the payer for payment, and handle all the paperwork. Many people seem to feel no responsibility for managing their own healthcare, and often also take little personal responsibility for their own lifestyle decisions. Many people have few skills in self-management of common and simple health problems. They want a pill for every symptom, instead of developing and using free self-care techniques. Perhaps we in the medical community have wanted it this way. If people are helpless and look to medicine to cure all their ills, we doctors will never be out of work! Unfortunately, this approach also contributes to the ever-escalating costs of health care.

The flip side of this individual disempowerment is the attitude some patients experience with their doctors. I met with a new patient recently who came with a number of questions about her current medical regimen. She had asked her previous doctor about the various options she might have, and if some additional testing might be in order, based on reading she had been doing. She said her doctor told her she was "too involved" with her own health care and she should leave those types of decisions to him. Some of us physicians would apparently rather have the patient be uninformed and unconcerned about their health, so that we can be "in charge." I think this is the medicine of the past, not of the future.

Our current prevailing health care payment system has removed most responsibility from the individual. It seems to assume that most patients are too unintelligent or unmotivated to make their own health care decisions, and often seems to treat physicians as if we are crooks always looking for ways to defraud the payer. This approach does not value the integrity of the doctor or patient, and ultimately hinders the likelihood of developing a true therapeutic relationship between them. When there is a direct financial covenant between the doctor and patient, some important things happen. The doctor truly feels responsible to give his or her best – this patient is actually paying good money for that doctor's services. The doctor cannot hide behind a big impersonal bureaucracy to deflect the doctor's direct personal commitment to serving the patient. The patient has an understanding for the costs of health care and the value of the doctor's time and expertise. I have had patients smile as they pay their bill, saying "what a bargain." I have had patients tell my office staff that they wrote a bigger check the previous day to the veterinarian for their dog's health problems. Patients need to see health care costs in the context of their whole lives –

compared to other services, food, utilities, gasoline for the car, and so forth.

Confronting the Fee Schedule

So, the first part of my confronting the payment conundrum was to determine what a fair price for my services was; and then not negotiate down for the purpose of achieving a volume of patients. It seemed risky at the time, but it is working. My patients are not in the poorhouse, I am making a decent living, and there is a 3 to 4-month wait for new patients to enter my practice. People want this sort of care, and are willing to pay for it, and often wait for it.

Unfortunately, not everyone is able to cover the cost of his or her health care. They may have no insurance, limited financial resources, or a type of health plan that does not reimburse them for any care the plan has not already chosen for them. The person may have a public assistance plan or Medicare, which may limit severely the choices he or she is able to make. Some suggestions to address these important issues of the uninsured and underinsured are discussed in Chapter 3.

There are other problems I see with my type of practice. The wait to see me as a new patient is way too long. That must mean there are too few doctors practicing personalized care that creates a direct covenant between physician and patient. We need to find ways for more paradigm pioneers to come forth, and to develop better roadmaps so the settlers will begin to join us in greater numbers. People want this kind of personalized care, and we doctors have to figure out more and better ways to deliver it. More of us may need to get out of the "treadmill" types of practices where other people tell us how many patients to see per hour or day, and begin to set our own priorities and schedules. We may need to be content with less income, in exchange for a much more satisfying life. But isn't that what this book is all about? Be the change.

I have also had patients who realized after seeing me for some period of time, they really could not afford the expense of paying for my services as an out-of-network provider. They have asked for my recommendations for a physician who is in their network, and we arrange to send their medical record to that person. I have a number of patients who see their in-network doctor for routine care, and visit me when their problem requires more time. I have even had some patients referred to me by their regular PCP in order to have someone take a look at their problem from a different perspective.

This scenario creates a more complicated "patchwork quilt" of care, and more communication between the patient, myself and the other doctor(s) is required, but it can work. And it speaks to the needed change in our system where we figure out a way to pay equitably for a doctor's time to consult with the patient, answer their questions, and consider them in a larger "holistic" view, than just the single stated reason for that specific visit. (My friend Laura told me her family doctor's office actually has a sign in the waiting room informing patients that they can only bring up one complaint in each visit!)

Until we have a system that allows doctors to spend the amount of time needed to address each patient's concerns fully by reimbursing them appropriately for their time, we will continue our current "band-aid" approach to health care that is not serving us well.

Slowing Down

Another portion of my own confrontation of a "system out of control" has been to slow down. I wanted to slow the pace of a typical high volume primary care practice and spend more time with each patient and more time with myself. I decided that seeing more people in order to either feel productive (i.e. "legitimate") or make more money was a sure path to burnout for me. As one of my favorite patients has said, "We have to learn to slow dance."

Starting a little later in the morning, taking 90 minutes for lunch, scheduling a full hour for new patients has felt like a luxury. I'm taking walks or swimming in the mornings, sitting for a few minutes with my husband, eating breakfast. I try to meditate or do some energy building Qi Gong exercises daily. I relax in comfortable chairs in my office with new patients to really hear their story. I see 10 to 20 patients in an average full day. I used to brag about being able to see 20 patients in a morning. And that was the model I once helped teach to students and residents. "Be efficient." "Learn good time management." These are important lessons, but so is the time-honored rule that "the patient will tell you the diagnosis if you just listen properly." We teach students that the foundation of good medicine is a full history. Then we show them practices where the doctor may be allowed 6 to 10 minutes for a returning patient, and 20 or 30 minutes for a new patient, if they are lucky. We often do not actually practice what we preach, or teach.

As I settled in to finish this book at a lovely retreat center called Shanitvanum outside Kansas City, I met a woman in her early 60's who was also on a personal retreat. When she found out I was a physician, she commented that it was so unusual to see a doctor actually taking care of herself and going to a retreat center for a few days. Isn't it a sad commentary that the public sees us doctors as so stressed and overly busy that they can't imagine us actually taking time to care for ourselves? Maybe eventually we can become the ones to set the model for self care.

Since I have slowed down, my overall health and happiness quotient have improved. I treasure every day more and feel truly enriched by most of my interactions with people.

Being Present

Being fully "present" with each patient takes concentration and energy. I learned from my non-physician colleagues early on that this "full presence" approach to interaction requires the practitioner to be very mindful regarding one's own care. We have to get enough rest and enough balance in life to do a good job and be fully present with each patient every day, especially when they are paying us real money for real service.

Too often I have heard stories from patients, and even experienced myself excessive waits for doctor's appointments – occasionally up to 2 and even 3 hours beyond the scheduled appointment time. In no other service industry would such rude disregard for the value of another's time be tolerated. Too often I have listened to patients who have told of a doctor's hurry to get out of the exam room as quickly as possible; so quickly that the actual reason for the visit is never revealed or dealt with. And in the past, I have been that doctor, with too many patients scheduled in a day, and too little time allotted to each for a full airing of their problems and worries.

Amy, a 35-year old patient, relayed a story to me that was very telling. She had the unfortunate need to have a hysterectomy at age 32, and was very sad that she would not be able to have children. In visits to various gynecologists she found it devastating to be asked several times when her last period was, or if she was pregnant – the doctors had not reviewed her chart to see that she had just had a hysterectomy.

I can't help but believe that this rushed approach to health care is not in the patient's best interest nor in the doctor's either. And not in terms of health care costs, as people then have to make more appointments, or see additional providers because their needs are not being met, or the doctor orders tests and consultations or medication prescriptions to manage symptoms because he or she does not have time to get a clear story of the problem, or counsel the person properly on ways to manage their problem without drugs. And because we often do not have time to develop an understanding with patients and build mutual trust, doctors order possibly unnecessary tests in order to be sure they are not missing anything for which they might be sued later.

This behavior does nothing to help control the costs of health care, but contributes to their continued escalation. In fact, an important article on this very subject was published in the Annals of Family Medicine in September/October 2005. In this study, the investigators found that physicians who used a patient-centered communication approach (open-ended questions, fewer interruptions by the physician, patient perception of being understood and receiving a clear explanation from the physician) spent less money in diagnostic testing than physicians who did not use such an approach.

My patient Helen went into menopause at a very young age. She experienced terrible sleep problems and was dismissed by her gynecologist as someone with a psychiatric issue. A psychiatrist diagnosed her as bipolar. She herself felt she had some kind of hormonal problem, and when tested was clearly suffering from imbalanced hormones. When a doctor finally listened to her fully, took her concerns seriously and approached her care with respect, she has done well. So many patients have mentioned to me the problems they have had with doctors not listening to them and taking them seriously, particularly when they have questions, or the doctor has perceived that their medical judgment is being questioned, and dismissed the patient as being "difficult."

I have also heard many stories of improved healing occurring when a doctor offered hope or a human touch. Sallie, the mother of a son with juvenile rheumatoid arthritis applauds the doctors she has met over the years as being ones who truly partner with patients and their parents and are very accessible. She also recalled an experience with surgery when she was quite frightened, the doctor held her hand as she was being anesthetized and she felt secure and warm because of that caring human gesture. Another woman told me a heartwarming story of a nurse who stayed with her as she was undergoing anesthesia, and that this simple act of human kindness made her feel safe and cared for. These examples of genuine human caring are what we all want in our health care experience. And they are so simple, and inexpensive. Why can't we experience this little extra effort every time we are in need of support?

Non-traditional Treatment Options

I have also been trying some new techniques I did not learn in medical school, residency or mainstream continuing education programs. I'm learning more about nutrition, acupuncture, yoga, special chiropractic techniques, new uses for older medicines, and finding people in my community who are skilled in the areas in which I am not capable. I feel I am getting back to the roots of medicine and enjoying each encounter with patients and each day more than I ever have before. I am rarely drained and exhausted at the end of the day. I feel happy and usually wake up looking forward to the new day with a bit of excitement.

Not only am I finding the heart and soul of medicine again, and rediscovering myself as a valuable person, but patients seem to be benefiting as well. I have received numerous notes, phone messages and letters of appreciation from patients.   (I have been fired by one or two as well.) Overall, the response to a practice style that allows time for giving and receiving the full story a patient has to tell has been very therapeutic for the patient, and gratifying for me. Comments such as "I've never had a doctor sit and listen to me like this." "After talking with you, telling my story, it's clear to me what I have to do." "Thank you for being an oasis in health care." "Your center is a blessing in my life." "Thank you for your time and patience, for being real and for treating me with respect." "It meant so much to be listened to and taken seriously. Your hugs truly lifted my spirit and renewed my faith." "I am so glad to have found a doctor that has ears and a heart, as well as a brain."

These comments are not put forth here to blow my own horn, but to reveal how important is the time spent listening to the patient in order for the clinical encounter to be effective. Most good physicians take as much time as they can in order to do the best job they can. Unfortunately, they often work in environments that do not value this kind of deep interaction between the doctor and patient, or they are heavily overscheduled, or the patient does not feel he or she has been listened to, even if the doctor thinks he or she has been attentive. Every doctor has a heart and ears as well as a brain. Sometimes patients do not get the feeling we are using our whole selves to be fully present with them. That sort of connection is essential to real healing, and is something we must continue to teach, model and reward in our students, colleagues and ourselves. A system that does not honor a true doctor-patient therapeutic relationship is out of control. But only we physicians can reaffirm the critical importance of this connection.

CHAPTER 3

HUMANIZING OUR HEALTH CARE SYSTEM

We need a new model of health care. We need a model that guarantees access to basic services to everyone and freedom of choice and an expectation of individual responsibility on each person's part.

Nearly 50 million Americans in 2008 – a record high - lacked health insurance and were not eligible for Medicaid. This accounts now for over 15 percent of the American population. *Fifteen percent!* Many of these people are members of working families. Some of these people pay for their care out of pocket; many go without any health care at all. Every year the number of uninsured citizens climbs, and in recent years federal spending for safety net care has been declining. The Kaiser Family Foundation reported in November 2005 that the number of uninsured Americans increased by 4.6 million from 2001 to 2004, yet federal safety net spending per uninsured person fell from $546 to $498 during that same period. The situation for low-income Americans, and those employed in jobs that do not offer health insurance keeps getting worse. Many employers find they cannot afford health benefits for their employees, and in America, health coverage is generally obtained as an employment benefit.

This latter fact – health insurance in America as an employee benefit – is actually a quirk of relatively recent history, not a longstanding cultural tradition. During World War II there was a serious shortage of workers, as so many young men were in service overseas. The government placed a ban on raising wages, so employers had to come up with creative ways to attract employees that were not wage-based. They struck a brilliant plan – offer health insurance! Prior to WWII, there really was not much of a health insurance industry in America. Health care was not particularly expensive, we had few costly technologies available, and doctors were comfortably in the middle class, but were not in the stratosphere of high-income earners, as many are today.

No one could predict in the 1940's that health care costs would skyrocket so dramatically over the next several decades, and become the economic millstone around our collective necks that is beginning to literally bring down our economy. In 2005, health insurance premiums raised 9.2% (after 4 consecutive years of double digit increases) but still **three times** the increase in worker's wages in 2005. And we have become more and more aware of the pressures on industry to try to cut health benefits, or pass on more of the cost to workers. Some of the largest auto manufacturers are closing plants and cutting jobs because they can no longer afford to employ as many workers with costly health benefits. Other employers are offering high-deductible plans, or foregoing offering insurance at all, especially smaller employers. As a small employer myself, I have had to make that same decision, as premiums for a small group are prohibitively expensive.

What about Quality?

For all our American pride about the quality of our health care and the superiority of our technology, we do **not** have the best health statistics in the world, yet we have the greatest cost. In 2002 – the latest year for which this data exists - the World Health Organization ranking showed that the United States was number 24 in life expectancy (Japan was number 1); while we spent $4,187 per capita in annual health expenditures Japan spent $2,373. "Per capita', of course, means an average of dollars spent per year when divided by the entire population. Some of us have much higher expenditures than others, who may have very few costs in a given year. My husband and I spend about $20,000 a year out-of-pocket on health insurance premiums, deductibles and co-pays, prescription drugs, dental and eye care and unreimbursed medical expenses (such as massage, chiropractic care, supplements and so forth) even though he is well insured through his employer, and I have no serious illnesses. I have patients in my practice who report paying $10-20,000 annually for premiums alone.

We also hear about a higher rate of quality problems in both hospital and office care in the U.S. compared with other nations, as well as more disorganization and higher costs when compared to Germany, Australia, Canada, New Zealand and Great Britain. The Commonwealth Fund reported in November 2005 results of a cross-national survey of patients' experiences with the health care system. Thirty-four percent of Americans reported errors such as receiving the wrong medication or dose, incorrect test results, a mistake in their treatment or being notified late of an abnormal result. Between 20 and 30% of patients from the other countries reported similar errors.

In 2001 the Institute of Medicine issued two landmark reports on health care safety and quality: *To Err is Human* and *Crossing the Quality Chasm*. They reported on the number of avoidable deaths in US hospitals due to human errors, and set an agenda for quality improvement in American health care. In 2004, the Institute for Healthcare Improvement (IHI) launched the "100,000 Lives Campaign" – a national initiative designed to save 100,000 lives in US hospitals by June 14, 2006. The goal is for all the 5,759 hospitals in the country to implement up to 6 "system" interventions that have been shown to be beneficial in improving care and saving lives. These changes include rapid response teams that can be called *before* a cardiac arrest occurs; delivering evidence-based care for heart attacks; preventing adverse drug interactions through careful medication review; preventing infections in intravenous catheters and surgical sites; and preventing pneumonia that can occur when patients are on ventilators. These changes sort of seem like things we should already be doing, don't they? The fact that we have to create new mechanisms to assure they are done every time with every patient highlights the problems we have in our overall healthcare system: nurses and doctors are often too busy to be able to do the kind of accurate job we (and they) expect, and we have inadequate systems in place to support them to do their jobs right every time. Whether this goal of preventing 100,000 deaths in hospitals is reached remains to be seen, but at least serious efforts are underway to look at processes in hospitals that support safer care.

But back to the important question of access to care: the U.S. was rated 54th in "financial fairness," by the World Health Organization (WHO) measured by the equal distribution of health costs faced by each household (Colombia was number 1.) And while France was ranked number one in overall health system performance, the U.S. was 37th, in spite of our spending the <u>most</u> money per capita for health care of any country in the world. We **are** ranked first in "responsiveness" – respect for the dignity of individuals, confidentiality of health records, prompt attention in emergencies, and choice of provider.

How can we retain this last item of great importance to our culture, 'responsiveness,' while improving health statistics such as life expectancy and infant mortality and improving the error rate in US healthcare? And how can we improve our "financial fairness" and equitable access to necessary services? These are the critical questions of our time.

Health Savings Accounts?

Perhaps employers should not actually provide insurance, but something like vouchers or even cash for employees to purchase an option that meets their particular needs. If every person in our country had a catastrophic, high deductible insurance plan in order to cover large (and usually unexpected) expenses, then had a medical IRA (or Medical Savings Account – an MSA, or most recently a Health Savings Account – an HSA) for all routine and preventive care, minor acute care and stable chronic care, people would need to be responsible for choosing their providers and paying their own bills for non-catastrophic care. The money placed in the HSA can only be used for a medically related expense, and not diverted for other uses. And the list of legitimate health expenses as approved by the IRS includes acupuncture, physical therapy, massage therapy, nutrient supplements, and other options currently not generally covered by insurance.

If we had this sort of arrangement, we would actually return to the concept of "insurance." Buying insurance means purchasing a policy to protect us in case of an unanticipated disaster, but we must budget for predictable, ongoing costs such as food, car repairs, gasoline, rent, clothing, etc. We buy auto insurance in case we are in an accident, not to cover gas, oil, and new windshield wipers: we budget for that sort of ongoing expense. Our current health care payment system is really not insurance so much as a "defined benefit" plan, and this arrangement institutionalizes a total disconnect between the cost of health care and the services rendered.

Imagine going to the grocery store, telling the clerk you are hungry, being given a cartload of food you did not select, and then some weeks or months later receiving a bill for "consumer's share/co-payment not covered by insurance." There is no itemized list of what each food item cost. Some of the food in the basket you enjoyed, and other items were not tasty to you or made you sick. You go to the store the next month and demand a cartful of the food you liked and none of the nasty items that made you ill and you are told that your food insurance company will not allow that choice. You must take the cartload they give you and eventually pay for some portion of it, even though you had no choice in its selection, and no idea of what any of the items cost.

No one would stand for such a scenario. Yet we are accepting this insanity in health care. If we have a managed care plan, we go to a doctor selected from a list of authorized providers, pay a $10 or $20 co-pay, tell the doctor our problem, and are given some suggestions for treating our problem, or a prescription, or perhaps some tests. We have no idea what these items actually cost. Perhaps a few weeks later we get a statement with little detail that tells us we have not yet met this year's deductible and owe the doctor $37.50 (or maybe $400.) Usually we just pay it, but there is no relationship between anything that happened a few weeks ago in the office and the money we are shelling out today. We have no concept of the cost of any service, and assume "my insurance will cover it."

Currently, too many entities outside the doctor-patient relationship are making the important decisions. Employers are choosing the most affordable plans and the plans dictate our choice of doctors and hospitals. The plans determine what drugs will be paid for and all other covered services. Plans usually determine the price to be paid for services, and negotiate to find the lowest bidders.

In my practice patients receive a bill at the time of service for their office care. They actually see the cost of various services, and decide if these services seem worth the cost to them. For some people, it is the first time they have ever had a sense of the actual cost of a health service. They are given a form to submit to their insurance company for reimbursement, which we explain in detail prior to their first appointment with me. Some patients decide not to come under this arrangement where they pay at the time of service and get reimbursed later. They need to go to a doctor on their health plan so that they have no up-front costs and do not have to actually file the insurance themselves. I completely understand and respect this situation, but have decided for my own practice I will not be the intermediary between the patient and the payer.

Using this payment arrangement, I have had many more meaningful discussions with patients about the cost versus value of a test or procedure than I did when practicing in a more conventional insurance-based way. Even if the person has an MSA or HSA or their insurance will be reimbursing them for most of the cost for my visit, they at least know how much my time is worth, what an EKG costs, what each lab test costs. If people really had to be responsible for all of their routine health care costs, they might make different choices. They might opt for more self-care, more prevention and less use of doctors and emergency rooms for minor and self-limited problems. They might decide that eating properly and getting exercise was cheaper in the long run than expensive medicines and doctor visits to manage their high blood pressure and diabetes.

Second, doctors and other providers would not have to wait for the insurance company to pay them, and patients would not have to have cash on hand in order to get care. The patient could use his or her HSA debit card or dedicated HSA checking account at the time of service, the money in such an account having been deposited either by the patient him or herself, or by their employer, or by the government for certain groups.

Third, employers would get out of the business of managing health care costs and benefits, and dealing with all the issues of healthcare economics. They would only have to cope with questions of how much salary to pay an individual, how much to contribute toward the employee's own purchase of insurance, or how much to contribute to their employee's health savings account. Employers could put the dollars they now spend for health insurance premiums toward the purchase of high deductible insurance policies, or put money into the employee's HSA. This makes health insurance fully portable and gets the employer out of the business of managing health care costs and having to actually purchase the insurance plan. It puts more responsibility on the employee to save and be a responsible consumer of health care.

Health Insurance That Stays With the Patient, Not the Employer

The "portability" issue is extremely important. So many people have had the experience of changing jobs and therefore changing health plans which then exclude them because they have a "pre-existing condition." This happened to me during medical school many years ago. I had health insurance purchased through the student health service. It was a requirement that all students be covered by this policy or by a family policy if eligible.

I was too old to be on my parents' policy, so purchased the mandated insurance. I developed a nodule in my thyroid. I had several tests. A few months later it was decided that I should undergo surgery to remove half of my thyroid gland, and I did so a few weeks later during a school break. Unfortunately, the academic year had changed just before my surgery, and the student health service had changed health plans at that time. The new plan determined that my thyroid problem was pre-existing their coverage of me, so denied paying for the surgery. No one at the university was able to get this decision overturned. As I was a student, the hospital and surgeon worked with me on discounting the bill and allowing payment over time. However, this experience brought right home the issue of "portability." I had no voice in my insurance plan being changed, I had to purchase that insurance as a requirement of enrollment and others outside of my control made the decision to change plans. If I had personally owned my own insurance, this problem of a pre-existing condition would have been eliminated.

I can scarcely keep track of the number of people I know – friends, patients and even a few colleagues – who are in jobs they dislike but cannot leave because they have a health problem that will be excluded as a "pre-existing" condition when they change employers and therefore health plans. Health care ends up determining so many important aspects of our lives – such as what job to take, or whether to change jobs or even careers.

According to data published by the U.S. Census Bureau, in 2006 most people had health insurance purchased and chosen by employers: 60%. Some 27% of people had coverage through a federal plan, 9% were self-insured and 15% uninsured. But employers are increasingly concerned about the viability of their companies given the continuously rising cost of health benefits.

According to the Kaiser Family Foundation, a non-profit health care think tank in Washington, DC, the average family health care premium rose 114% from 2000 to 2010 ($6,400 to $13,770). The portion of employer-sponsored insurance paid by the employee has risen by an even more dramatic 147% from $1,619 to $3,997 annually during the same ten years. In 2010 the employee paid, on average, $9,773 for family coverage.

Another headline in the June 23, 2005 *USA Today* described the problems General Motors has in being able to afford the continually rising cost of health care for its employees. According to that article, GM spends more money per car on health care than on steel. In competitor countries where health care is a universal benefit of citizenship and not paid for by employers, the costs of many products – including automobiles - is markedly lower, thus contributing to the imbalance of trade we see today in America: more goods come in to our country than are exported, and ultimately our national bottom line suffers.

The difficulty employers have in paying the costs of health care for workers gives us another reason why so many working Americans and their families live without health insurance – the breadwinner can't find a full time job with benefits, so has to cobble together several part time positions to make ends meet, none providing insurance benefits.

High Administrative Overhead

If the profit motive for third parties who do not provide any direct service but just manage the health care plan were eliminated from the scenario, significant financial savings could result. It is estimated by Physicians for a National Health Plan (PHNP) that in a for-profit health system, between 19 and 30% of the total revenue is spent on administrative overhead. In a non-profit environment this figure averages 13%. For Medicare, administrative overhead is about 3%, while in the Canadian health insurance program it is 1%. A report in *Health Affairs* in November 2005 showed that billing and insurance paperwork consumes one-fifth of California's privately insured health spending, amounting to $26 billion annually. If the state adopted a single payer insurance system, effectively eliminating a vast amount of paperwork, $18 to $21 billion could be saved annually.

We all have heard stories of the seven-figure-plus incomes of some health plan CEO's. Most of us think this is obscene. If the corporate profit motive were eliminated from the system, more money would be available to provide care. Less time and energy would be spent trying to bolster corporate and shareholder profits, and more to giving service. A significant shift has occurred in the growth of the for-profit sector in managed care: 46% of patients enrolled in HMO's in 1989 were in a for-profit system. By 1999 that figure had grown to 64%. In 2006 fewer people overall were enrolled in HMO's, but most of these are still for-profit organizations. As that figure increased in the late 1990's, so did discontent with HMO care and a movement began where patients are now able to sue their HMO for blocking the ability to receive needed care based on cost. These issue impact even non-HMO insurance organizations who use cost to justify restriction of care.

Employers who choose health plans for their workers are beginning to get very nervous. If patients can sue their HMO, they could also sue the entity that selected the plan in the first place – i.e. the employer. Patient choice and autonomy in selecting a health plan begins to look better and better to many employers.

HSA – the Ideal Solution?

A moment about the down side of HSA's. In the current environment, most of the people who select HSA's are relatively healthy and have an income which allows them to invest the $1,000-$3,000 deductible into the HSA account. These people are then removed from what is called a "risk pool" – or the large body of relatively healthy people who do not cost much in insurance payments, so their premiums help cover the higher costs that the sicker members of the population expend. The larger the "risk pool" and the more relatively healthy people in it, the less risk an insurance company takes to provide an insurance product. Some insurance companies refuse to offer insurance to the disabled or those with serious or chronic health problems, or offer premiums that are horribly expensive. The only way to make an HSA plan workable is to enroll virtually everyone in it. Then the high deductible catastrophic plan (the actual "insurance" portion) has a risk of expenditure spread over a very large population and the premiums for everyone are affordable.

That means also that everyone has an HSA account for discretionary spending of the deductible amount. Employers could find contributing to this health savings account an attractive employee benefit.

For low income, unemployed, underemployed, disabled, and other medically disenfranchised citizens, the government could actually contribute money to an HSA or provide vouchers that allow people to use facilities and providers of their choice for defined services. We know that adults who go without insurance for long periods have many unmet health care needs, and that more patients in the U.S. forgo needed health care because of cost than in the U.K., Canada, Australia or New Zealand according to a 2005 survey conducted by the Commonwealth Fund.

The vouchers – which could be used as if they were cash for the deductible portion of the HSA - would cover specific services only - such as prenatal care, well child care, routine preventive services for adults and children, immunizations, and care for acute and chronic health problems. This system could work similarly to food stamps, where recipients shop where they wish, and have choices of food to buy, but the vouchers cover only essential nutritional items, not champagne and caviar or cigarettes. We could call these health care vouchers "medical stamps."

Health Care Rationing

I keep making health care analogies to food and grocery stores. Is health care like food? Everyone needs a certain amount of each in order to survive and thrive. Some get too much food and are obese; some get too much health care and are over-medicated or suffer from procedure- or drug-induced complications. Some people get too little food and are malnourished; some get too little medical care and are sick or ailing. People with limited means can be eligible for government assistance through food stamps, food banks, food kitchens, etc. They can be eligible as well for Medicaid, free clinics, and other charity care.

Those who can afford face-lifts, tummy tucks, and refractive surgery can get them. Those who can afford caviar, champagne and filet mignon can get them. We do have income disparities in our society, and some people have more "goodies" than others. While many of us feel that health care should be a right, we have never been willing to define how much is a right, and which health services are "luxuries." At the extreme ends of the spectrum, the distinction is easy. Prenatal care and immunizations are necessities, and the costs are clearly beneficial to society as well as the individual. Face-lifts and refractive surgery are luxuries that no government program would be required to provide. What gets very difficult is the multitude of possibilities closer to the center: organ transplants, expensive intensive care for terminally ill persons, unproven expensive treatments for cancer, and the list goes on and on. As a society, we have not yet been able to confront these gray zones very well. Yet we are all angry when the managed care company tries to define them for us. And we *really* want to avoid the word "rationing." Unfortunately, resources actually are finite, and some kind of rationing will always occur.

Public Debates on Priorities in Health Care (Otherwise Known as "Rationing")

During the 1990's, the state of Oregon undertook open debates about health care rationing within the state's Medicaid program. Public forums were convened to discuss the reality of the actual amount of money available in the system, and created a prioritized list of services that could be offered. Money would be expended for the high priority items, and when the budget was exhausted, the lower priority procedures would not be covered.

This open, public discussion, debate and articulation of values and fiscal realities is the only ethical way to ration care. What is more commonly encountered regarding rationing is that an insurer develops guidelines for what may be covered or not, but the details are unclear and not openly stated. A person usually finds out that a potential life-saving procedure or drug is not covered only when it has been denied.

Howard Brody, MD, a family physician and ethicist at the University of Texas Medical Branch, has been very forthcoming about the reality of rationing health care, and how to ethically do so. His view is the one stated above: An open articulation of values and fiscal restraints, with a public declaration of priorities and limits is the key to fair rationing. As a society, we need to state what will be covered in any system of payment (be it public, universal health care, or private insurance) and what will not. It is not the individual doctor's role to ration care, nor is it the insurance company's role. It is the public's role and responsibility to determine our society's priorities in health care, and then be willing to face the fiscal obligation to pay for those priorities.

Health Care as a Right

Back to the analogy of food and health care: employers don't give employees a food allowance and require them to shop only at one designated grocery chain, which then decides what foods will be available, how fresh the food is, and so forth. People budget for food and buy what they want where they want within their budget.

Is health care a right any more than food is a right? I don't know. There is survival value assignable to both. Healthy people in healthy societies need access to both. However, a fundamental problem in our culture is that we never have really defined "health care." And we have this problem of articulating how much and what type of health care is a "right." Wants and needs always exceed resources, even in wealthy societies such as ours, so some form of rationing is inevitable.

More individual autonomy and responsibility might help us get around this issue as well. If people can spend the money in their HSA on any service they deem useful to their health, then the payer's definition is less relevant. If a person feels that chiropractic treatment and acupuncture are beneficial in managing his or her back pain, that person is entitled to spend the HSA money on those services. If that person decides to see an MD for an evaluation and an MRI is recommended, the patient can engage in a meaningful discussion about the potential benefits of an expensive test like an MRI, and ultimately decide how to spend that health care money. And if doctors, chiropractors and acupuncturists all communicated with one another in an integrated system, any patient who really needs an MRI would get one, regardless of where he or she entered the system. Each practitioner would be aware of the skills and contributions of the others, and patients would be directed to the proper care at the proper time. A more detailed discussion on this concept of integrating mainstream and complementary care is found in Chapter 4.

Perhaps food is not a perfect analogy. Most people understand food and are familiar with what they want and need. Health care is different. Understanding what a given symptom may mean, and knowing how to properly decide on which tests and treatments may be needed requires extensive training and experience in most situations. And the public generally trusts that doctors and other health care professionals will act in the patient's best interest to find the proper diagnosis and treatment options. The issues we face in health care are usually of a higher complexity of decision-making and information-seeking than are food choices and options.

We generally have no food "emergencies" unless we lose our job or our income drops substantially. We do have the possibility for health emergencies, which could unexpectedly cost us dearly. This is the reason to have insurance. How to provide that insurance, who pays for it, what is covered and freedom of choice are the issues at hand.

"Consumer-Driven Health Care"

There is a groundswell of interest in what is being called "consumer-driven" health care, where patients themselves choose their health plans. A new industry is developing to provide information and enrollment over the Internet directly to consumers. Everything from facelifts to prenatal care will be marketed publicly on the Web, and the public will begin to get a sense of the variety in costs of various services. Health insurance options will also be marketed and sold in this way, and competition will flourish. The public will presumably become increasingly sophisticated purchasers of insurance and of direct medical services, as medical groups and hospitals begin to openly compete in a true open market format – directly to patients. For now, only about 17% of employers offer any choice of plans to employees. But many health economy pundits predict this scenario will be changing in the near future. In fact, high deductible insurance plans with the MSA/HSA component are growing rapidly. In 2005, only about 1% of all covered employees were enrolled in these consumer-directed plans. By 2010, that number was 13%, according to the Kaiser Family Foundation.

For those persons covered by a government voucher or "medical stamp" program, some aspects of this same scenario could apply. There could be a catastrophic plan for unexpected high cost illness or injuries, but the person her/himself could be responsible for the expenditure of the medical stamps, as one is are for food stamps. If the HSA concept takes hold, then money could even be put into a special HSA for such individuals, and they could then direct how they choose to spend those dollars.

Other Reform Proposals

The American Medical Association (AMA) has put forth a health insurance reform proposal. It centers also on individually-owned health insurance that are fully portable, with tax incentives designed to make premiums more affordable and expand coverage to include many more Americans in the insurance market than currently can afford to be. The AMA plan is quite vague, and does not offer universal coverage.

Physicians for a National Health Plan has long advocated a single-payer system, much like the Canadian system. Their plan would cover all Americans for necessary medical care by expanding and improving Medicare, and be funded by savings incurred with the elimination of the high overhead and profits of the private insurance industry.

The American Academy of Family Physicians supports universal coverage for all Americans that includes **no** co-payment for designated preventive services, and a maximum 20% co-pay for most outpatient services, including mental health care. Out-of-pocket expenses would be capped; the current insurance market would be retained, with public/private oversight and funding via a national tax.

Many health economists and political pundits have suggested other scenarios. While the most equitable and sensible proposal really is a national single-payer plan, there has been no groundswell of support as yet for this kind of proposal by either major political party in the US, or by any large consumer group. It looks as if everyone wants the system to be "fixed", but they'd prefer it not cost more or require any of us to actually change. But.....

A New Philosophy

The changes suggested by this book will require us to think and behave differently. Can't we, as a society, agree that all of our citizens shall have access to some set of basic services, for which all of us will share in paying? Can't we develop a mechanism for defining these services and making them universally available?

All of us will have to become more comfortable with the reality that there are finite limits to what each of us can afford personally and what we as a larger society can afford. While we have technology to do miraculous things, we may not always be able to afford those miracles. And there will always be some who can afford them, and some who cannot. When we decide to deal out the public dollar, limits will have to be set. We will have to get more comfortable with such limits, and we must be willing to engage in open discussions about them, so that the inevitable rationing that must occur will at least be ethical, as Howard Brody suggests.

I recall as a child in the 1960's seeing a special TV documentary that reported on the discussions undertaken to decide which individuals would receive kidney dialysis, and which would not. The latter would die without that needed treatment. But dialysis then was very expensive, not widely available, and offered only to patients who met certain criteria. A committee was convened to discuss and evaluate the details of each case and decide who was most likely to benefit from treatment. This was my first exposure to "rationing" of health care. 'Rationing' is a term that no one in America wants to hear or utter. It is usually used in a derogatory sense when discussing care provided in countries that have universal access, with articulated limits – so-called "socialized medicine." What few of us in America want to face is that we have *de facto* rationing – rationing by means of a person's individual ability to pay, or by hidden decisions on coverage made by insurance companies behind closed doors.

Now some of the insurers are also practicing rationing as well, by denying services they believe are too expensive for the benefit gained. We rail against this. If there is a treatment available, we want it - hang the cost! Our lack of understanding about the costs of care, and our naïve idea that we are entitled to everything has led us down this path of denying the reality of limits.

Another Personal Story – Limits for *ME??*

When my husband was diagnosed with multiple myeloma - a type of bone marrow cancer - in 2001, we were covered by a very good health plan through his employer. He was able to receive excellent care from our local oncologists and bone marrow transplant team, including a second opinion from a specialist in this disease in Boston. He was able to undergo high dose chemotherapy and an autologous stem cell transplant (a process that harvests one's own bone marrow stem cells, then freezes them for reinfusion after the chemotherapy to "rescue" the destroyed bone marrow and allow it to grow new red cells, white cells, platelets and antibodies, and save the person's life. Rather a remarkable achievement of modern medicine!) In my husband's case, this procedure was very successful and we are so grateful that it was available to him, and that our insurance covered it.

The interesting, yet frightening wrinkle in this story is that my husband had actually quit his employed position only a month prior to his diagnosis, in order to start his own business. Fortunately because of COBRA regulations (Federal legislation passed in 1986) he was able to continue his previous insurance coverage for 18 months, as long as he continued to pay the full premium. Fortunately, the major portion of his expensive treatment was completed in this 18- month period.

However, once the COBRA clock ran out, he had to find private insurance as a self-employed individual. Now, of course, he had a" pre-existing condition", so that most companies would not insure him at all, or if they did, the premiums would be sky-high. Again, fortune smiled upon us. We live in Kansas, one of 34 states that mandate an insurance plan for these sorts of otherwise "uninsurable" people. There is one insurer, and it is rather expensive, but at least it exists. If this option had not been available to us, we would have had to pay for all his health expenses out-of-pocket until we became eligible for Medicaid – a very frightening and disheartening prospect. Yet many in our country face this problem daily.

In fact, the number one reason for personal bankruptcy in America is medical expenses. Sixty percent of all personal bankruptcies are due, at least in part, to illness or medical bills. Seventy-six percent of the people in medical bankruptcy had insurance at the time of their illness, according to *Health Affairs* in February 2005. Most of these people had been to college, had responsible jobs and had been homeowners.

If, at the time of my husband's diagnosis, we had a system of coverage in America where everyone was in the same "risk pool" and insurance was fully portable, we would not have had the uncertainty of finding health coverage at the very time we were unstable and worried about his serious health condition. And his former employer would not have sustained the high costs of his cancer treatment that undoubtedly raised their group premiums the following year.

The grim reality is that this sort of devastating diagnosis can happen to anyone at anytime. None of us is safe from the prospect of economic disaster if we have an unexpected health crisis, especially if we are in a period of employment change, or COBRA expiration, or we work in a job that offers no health benefits.

Fortunately, too, my husband has a kind of cancer for which there are some agreed-upon treatments that are considered standard care, and therefore are covered by the insurance plan. There are many experimental treatments also. It is not clear that his insurance would cover them if he ever needed such experimental therapy. The caring wife in me says, "I want him to have anything and everything that might help him." The realist in me knows that we cannot afford everything, "hang the costs." But I'd like to know there has been an explicit discussion that is open and public about what can be afforded in the system and what cannot, and why. Like anyone else, I want to know that the denial of care is not because the executive of the health care company needs a bigger raise, or the shareholders need a increase in the stock value of the company. I could understand foregoing expensive experimental treatment because it serves the greater good of our entire society that is covered by a universal health plan. My own family might have to be financially burdened if we opted to try expensive experimental treatments, and people without the same financial resources might have to forego the experiments. These are very tough realities. But denying that these realities exist and believing society can afford everything for everyone is a belief we each must change.

Victimhood

Finally, many of us have been behaving as if we are helpless victims of the "system." Doctors seem to feel they have to work within the time and resource constraints of managed care. Employers feel they have to keep providing health benefits. Health care executives feel they must always bend to Wall Street and the bottom line. We have to change, one at a time. We each have to decide, within ourselves, how we can do our job within our society in ways that allow us to sleep at night and use our talents well. I cannot tell anyone else how to act or how to work. My way will not be the way for everyone. But we each must face our own souls each morning in the mirror of our lives. Another wise suggestion from Gandhi seems apt:

"I ask nobody to follow me. Everyone should follow his own inner voice."

When we all follow our own inner voice our system will finally have become humanized.

CHAPTER 4

EMBRACING NEW HEALING METHODS

Interest and enthusiasm about unconventional healing methods is growing rapidly in our society. The public wants to see useful complementary therapies incorporated into mainstream medical care. More and more health professionals are seeking education about alternative healing methods, and formal training programs in "integrative medicine" are beginning to take hold.

David Eisenberg, a Harvard physician whose surveys on Americans' use of alternative therapies have opened the door to legitimate discussion, reported in 1998 that 42% of Americans were using some kind of alternative therapy or visiting an alternative health care practitioner. The National Center for Complementary and Alternative Medicine (NCCAM) of the NIH reported in 2007 that approximately 38% of American adults and 11.2% of children use some kind of CAM therapy. Consumer Reports surveyed 46,000 subscribers in 2000 and found that 60% who use alternative therapies told their doctors they were doing so. In fact, nearly one quarter of patients who tried an alternative therapy did so on the recommendation of a doctor or nurse.

Andrew Weil, MD, one of the most visible forces in American medicine today working to bring alternative and conventional medicine together, developed the first integrative medicine training program for physicians in the U.S. According to Dr. Weil, integrative medicine is healing oriented and scientifically influenced, humanistic, individual-based medicine. It "... combines the best ideas and practices of alternative and conventional medicine in order to maximize the body's innate potential for self-healing – it is not simply about doctors learning to prescribe herbs or...acupuncture in addition to or instead of pharmaceutical drugs. Rather, integrative medicine involves a partnership in which the patients and practitioner together address healing on all levels: physical, psychological and spiritual." It also includes all aspects of a person's lifestyle and emphasizes the therapeutic relationship between doctor and patient. Dr. Weil further asserts, "...the integrative medicine movement is about nothing less than the transformation of medicine."

Are we ready for this transformation? I think we are. The distress we are feeling about our whole delivery system helps us become ripe for change. The fact that too many citizens are disenfranchised from health care creates an environment looking for reform. And new information and openness about unconventional approaches to healing all combine to create fertile ground for a dramatic transformation in health care. Dr. Weil feels one major impetus for this integrative medicine movement is the "growing gulf between what consumers want and what doctors are trained to do. Consumers want doctors who have the time to help them understand the nature of their medical problems; who will not push drugs and surgery as the only treatment options; who are aware of nutritional influences on health and can answer intelligently questions about dietary supplements; who are sensitive to mind-body interactions and able to see patients as more than just physical bodies; and who will not laugh at them for bringing up topics like Chinese medicine and homeopathy."

Lack of Success with Chronic Conditions

One of the main reasons people seek care from "complementary" providers is that they are experiencing problems with chronic conditions for which mainstream medicine has not helped them sufficiently. Chronic diseases (diabetes, arthritis, high blood pressure, asthma, heart disease, depression, etc.) are the ones for which we currently spend the most money in healthcare today. And payers, doctors, and many medical organizations are working hard to find new ways to "manage" these chronic conditions. Everything from self-care activities, group medical visits, streamlined flow sheets to track information in the doctor's office (or even on the internet for the patient), physician payment for performing the proper tests and procedures to monitor these conditions are all major areas of current investment in the healthcare system.

An entire new industry is actually cropping up called "Disease Management" companies. These groups focus on identifying and communicating regularly with patients who have serious chronic illnesses to enable them to better manage their condition. Revenues for these companies were reported at about

$600 million in 2002. By 2009, they earned approximately $2.5 billion! Some health plans have internal disease management entities, and these efforts at disease management for conditions such as diabetes, congestive heart failure, asthma and so forth are predicted to increase in the future, especially if current Medicare and other demonstration projects prove to provide both cost-savings and improved patient outcomes.

And to make matters even more complex, most primary care patients who have a chronic illness have more than one condition, making their care even more complicated. This problem of "multimorbidity" has not yet been well studied, and guidelines for care of such patients do not yet exist. We do have clinical guidelines for managing a person with diabetes and for managing asthma, as two examples. We do not, however, have guidelines for the proper management of multiple "co-morbid" conditions – diabetes and asthma in the same person, when medications might counteract one another, or monitoring for one condition may supersede monitoring the other. As a group of Canadian researchers pointed out in the *Annals of Family Medicine* in 2005, "patients with multimorbidity seen in family practice represent the rule, rather than the exception" and multiple morbidities increase with patient age. This fact complicates the practice of primary care, as any family physician or internist can report.

Researchers from Duke University published a paper in the same 2005 issue of *Annals of Family Medicine* in which they calculated the time it would take a primary care physician to perform all the recommended practice guidelines for the 10 most common chronic conditions seen in primary care. They concluded that performing these suggested activities would take more hours in a day than the physician has available for all patient care. Clearly our model of medical management is becoming outdated. We need new strategies, a bigger team to help, and more responsibility and tools given to the patient to actually manage his or her condition. And, we need to work much harder on preventing chronic disease in the first place. In the meantime, patients are seeking alternatives to help them manage their symptoms and disabilities.

Federal Funding for Complementary Medicine

The National Institutes of Health (NIH) are keenly aware of this public interest in unconventional approaches. The Office of Alternative Medicine at NIH was created in 1992, and subsequently elevated to Center status in 1999 – another step along the way to becoming a full-fledged "Institute". The National Center for Complementary and Alternative Medicine (NCCAM) had a research budget of about $80 million in 2000, growing to $128 million in 2010. While that is a small amount by NIH standards, it has increased every year. Centers for Alternative Medicine around the country are funded by NCCAM. Educational demonstration projects are also being funded, to bring conventional health professionals and alternative healers closer together. As we have more solid research about the usefulness of previously non-mainstream therapies, our ability to help patients will increase. As we vigorously examine those areas we have viewed as "alternative", we will also have to more rigorously evaluate our "mainstream" practices, and ultimately hold all healing methods to the same standard: proper evidence of effectiveness and safety.

The NIH is currently funding five areas of research interest: mind-body practices, bioelectric or energy medicine practices, alternative healing systems, body-based healing practices, and biologically-based practices (herbs, diets, nutritional supplements.) Many of these arenas already have substantial research over many years to support their efficacy for selected health problems. Meditation and biofeedback, for example, are two "mind-body" practices that have shown consistently beneficial results for treating hypertension, headache, chronic pain and stress-related disorders. However, these five research areas are considered "complementary and alternative" for three major reasons: they are not taught in U.S. allopathic (MD) medical schools, they are not generally offered in U.S. hospitals, and they are not usually paid for by insurance.

Mainstream "Allopathic Medicine"

To clarify a term I will be using over and over – "allopathic" medicine refers to the type of medicine MD students in the U.S. learn and what American MD's practice. "Allo" means "against" or "opposing", which is largely the type of medicine we practice: we give treatments to oppose disease: "*anti*-biotics", "*anti*-depressants", "*anti*-hypertensives" etc. Other medical systems may use different approaches: "*osteo*"-pathic medicine manipulates the musculoskeletal system to help overcome illness; "*homeo*pathy" uses a concept of similars to treat disease – "homeo" meaning "same." "Naturopathy" is a field that uses natural therapies – herbs and nutrients – to manage health and illness issues.

While some of these methods are offered in some hospitals (e.g. biofeedback and meditation interventions are offered in some pediatric and psychiatric units), in general, these five areas are not well integrated into mainstream medicine. "Diet and nutrition" is always an area I chuckle about when considering it an "alternative" therapy. Good nutrition is a mainstay of excellent health. But, it is poorly taught to MD students, food in hospitals is frequently not part of the patient's healing plan, and generally insurance does not cover nutrition and lifestyle programs. Therefore, it qualifies as "alternative."

Complementary and Alternative Medicine or "CAM"

Some of the most common complementary and alternative (often shortened to "CAM") practices that patients use are: prayer, herbs, chiropractic, massage, and vitamin therapies. Other common CAM therapies include homeopathy, acupuncture and Chinese medicine, yoga, naturopathy, Ayurvedic medicine, hypnosis. Many types of energy therapies are being utilized, but are less openly discussed by patients and practitioners: therapeutic touch, Reiki, magnet therapy, bioenergy therapy, and subtle energy therapy.

One question that I am frequently asked by my physician colleagues is "why do patients seek these alternative therapies? Their insurance doesn't usually cover them, and they can be really expensive." We all have stories about the patient who "cannot afford" her prescription medicines, but spends $200 on vitamins and supplements monthly. Physicians are sometimes confounded by this situation. The reality is that patients seek these CAM therapies and therapists for some basic reasons: CAM practitioners spend more time with patients – the average visit is 30 minutes. A high value is placed in a CAM interaction on healing, caring and partnership. Patients perceive this approach as more holistic, with their psychological and often spiritual health being addressed along with the physical aspects.

As mentioned above, patients also seek CAM practices for chronic health problems and those associated with aging, for which conventional medicine is less effective. Most patients who use CAM therapies also use conventional medicine. They turn to the CAM approach when the mainstream approach has failed them: chronic back pain, arthritis, some kinds of cancer, irritable bowel syndrome, chronic fatigue, fibromyalgia – all conditions which have limited options for relief in the conventional arena. They also turn to CAM therapies when conventional medicine has left them with a terminal condition and bereft of hope- few options for comfort and a dignified end of life and with no sense of dying in a state of peace and completion, just a feeling of hopelessness and often desperation.

A memorable patient comes to mind in this context. Gordon was dying of lung cancer, and his wife brought him to see me, desperate for some new "alternative" treatment to help his terminal situation. He himself seemed apathetic, and just sat silently, slumped on the couch, looking at the floor while she animatedly discussed a clinic in Germany she had heard of that was using a new kind of unconventional therapy for cancer. I first offered to look up this clinic on the Internet, but as I rose to go to the computer on my desk, I turned around and sat back down. I had reviewed Gordon's records and found he really did have very late stage, terminal lung cancer. To offer any additional treatments at this point seemed completely futile and actually unfair to him. He needed to complete his living on this earth, and leave with some sense of wholeness. I said to the couple "I am not sure that what I am going to say is what you came to hear, but there is such a thing as dying healed."

At this point, Gordon sat up straighter, and looked more alert. He asked "Healed? How's that?" I said "We all will die eventually and it looks as if your time is near. Have you completed all your legal papers and made your wishes known to your family? Have you forgiven anyone who needs to be forgiven, and have you sought forgiveness from anyone you might want it from? There are important things to do at the end of one's life, and you should be given the chance to do those things, not be distracted with running after useless treatments. I don't think this is what you came to see me for today, but this is what I can offer."

Gordon looked in my eyes and said, "This is exactly what I came for. Thank you." He passed away a few weeks later, having finished what he needed to do.

The Meaning of Healing

I have been using this term "healing" a lot so far in this book. I will be using it in upcoming chapters as well. What does it really mean? Does 'healing' mean 'curing'? Or does it mean something else? Many physicians, nurses, anthropologists, psychologists, theologians, philosophers and great thinkers have pondered this question over the centuries. The word "heal" means "to make sound or whole" and derives from the root "*hal*" or the state of being whole. *Hal* is also the root of the word "holy", defined as "spiritually pure." There always does seem to be a sense in the word "healing" that something almost spiritual is occurring during the healing process. And as the example of Gordon, the dying patient shows, there was no cure for his illness, but healing did occur. I believe he left my office feeling more 'whole' and at peace than when he came in.

Healing isn't something talked about on a regular basis in modern medicine. We strive for cures, effective "treatment", improvement in objective measures like blood pressure and cholesterol levels, and often relief of symptoms. And yet, healing remains a core function of medicine, and something people seek from physicians every day. Maybe this discrepancy between what we strive for as modern, scientific physicians (cure) and what patients are often seeking (wholeness) is a major source of so much discontent with modern medicine.

Thomas Egnew published in the *Annals of Family Medicine* in 2005 a synopsis of interviews with some of America's leading physicians who have conducted research and/or written about healing in medicine. The conclusions of his in-depth conversations with these seasoned physicians were summarized in the following way: "Healing may be operationally defined as the personal experience of the transcendence of suffering." Dr. Egnew discusses some impediments in current US health care that prevent this sort of healing encounter to seem relevant – such as episodic contact with specialty physicians and lack of continuity of care that generates a trusting relationship, and "the economics of primary care practice that force patient volumes in time increments that make the intimate connection necessary for healing difficult." He says "By helping patients transcend suffering, physicians surpass their curative roles to claim their heritage as healers." This statement indicates that healing is actually a higher calling than curing, and something physicians perhaps should aspire to, because patients need us to do so. Many CAM practitioners already are doing just this, and in the process have more patient visits per year than family doctors.

Integrating CAM and Conventional Care

As we gain more information and familiarity with unconventional practices, we will see patients being helped in ways conventional medicine falls short today. When we discover the right modality at the right time, we may be able to improve clinical outcomes, AND save money. If we use CAM therapies only as a "last resort" after all our conventional approaches have been tried and failed, we will potentially spend a great deal of effort, waste time, and use resources on ineffective treatments, when an effective "alternative" may be the correct intervention early in the course of a health problem. One example I like to use in this regard is with people who suffer a minor "whiplash" injury from a car accident or fall. If there is no significant structural abnormality (such as a slipped cervical disc), then a massage or acupuncture treatment as soon as possible may be the most effective way to relieve muscle spasm. Putting the person into a restraining collar and giving them antispasmodic medications – a fairly typical conventional medical approach - may only prolong their disability and pain.

We also need to keep in perspective the fact that modern allopathic medicine applies interventions that are powerful. Not only can we dramatically save lives with our drugs and surgery, but also we can cause complications, adverse reactions, and even death. As discussed in Chapter 3, The Institute of Medicine convened a blue ribbon panel to look into the serious problem of errors in medicine, stimulated by the data that approximately 100,000 people die in U.S. hospitals each year from adverse drug reactions and drug interactions alone. This is not to say that US hospitals are essentially dangerous places to be, but that very sick people are there who have serious health problems, and that it is humans who take care of them. These humans are capable of making errors, especially when they are overtired, understaffed, or not given the proper supports to do their difficult jobs effectively.

There are models of an integrative type of care being developed around the country. Dr. Weil's Program in Integrative Medicine at the University of Arizona was the first training program in a medical school to bring physician graduates together for a two year intensive training in understanding unconventional methods of healing, learning to practice some of these techniques themselves, and learning to work in a team effort with non-MD healers. The goal of this program has been to educate the academic leaders who can open similar programs in other medical schools around the country.

A number of hospitals and health systems have started nascent efforts at integrative medicine clinics or practices. Among the many notable ones are Pacific Medical Center and the University of California Medical Center in San Francisco; The Center for Health and Healing at New York's Beth Israel Hospital; Lutheran General Hospital in the Chicago area; and Sutter Health Care in California. Avera McKennan Health system in North Dakota has opened a new model of an integrative midlife women's health clinic where care is individualized and aspects of hormone balance, nutrition, lifestyle and mind-body connections are attended to.

Even some private group practices are beginning to integrate complementary therapies into their armamentarium. One example is California Cancer Care, a group of 5 oncologists in northern California that offers art therapy, massage, acupuncture, nutritional counseling, Jin Shin Jyutsu (a form of gentle Japanese bodywork) and guided imagery along with conventional cancer treatments.

My friend, Dr. Nancy Russell, was the first physician in the Kansas City area to open an integrative health center in the early 1990's. She works with several colleagues in various complementary fields in her office, and gave me invaluable advice when I contemplated opening the Sastun Center of Integrative Healthcare in 1998. The Sastun Center offers open-minded family medicine with a functional medicine approach, individualized help for women traversing the midlife hormonal and emotional transition, Chinese medicine (acupuncture and herbs), naturopathic medicine, massage and bodywork, bioenergy therapy, nutrition counseling and nutrient therapy, psychological counseling, group visits for chronic conditions, yoga classes (including therapeutic yoga for people with restricted mobility), and a variety of workshops and seminars on topics related to healing and self care. All the practitioners at our center meet together weekly to discuss cases and learn from one another.

Many medical schools are also developing such practices, and about half of the medical schools in the U.S. have developed some kind of curriculum in CAM therapies. Usually these are elective experiences, and often included because of student demand. As of April 2005, 64 of our nation's 125 allopathic (MD) medical schools offer specific elective courses in Complementary and Alternative Medicine, and 91 schools include CAM as part of required courses. None yet have a required course. Forty-two academic medical centers have joined together into an organization called the Consortium of Academic Centers in Integrative Medicine to promote more education and research in the integrative medicine arena.

Case Examples of Integrative Medicine Success

I can offer several examples of specific cases where integrating the best of conventional Western medicine and some complementary therapies resulted in excellent, and likely improved outcomes. My own husband found that if he had a massage before his chemotherapy treatments, he felt more relaxed and had less muscle pain and nausea. If he had a massage a day after the chemo, his body actually hurt more, possibly because the massage perhaps "pushed" the toxic chemicals into the muscles after the infusion.

I can recall the cases of two young boys, aged 6 and 8, who were experiencing enuresis (bedwetting) that was becoming a real problem for them and their families. The conventional approaches of behavior modification techniques had not helped, and their doctors were recommending medication to help the problem. In each case, a short course of acupuncture treatments completely resolved the bedwetting.

I have seen several cases of young children with significant hyperactive behavior problems be immediately calmed and focused after being give homeopathic treatment (See Glossary for clarification of this term), and innumerable patients with irritable bowel syndrome treated very effectively and safely with Chinese herbal medicine. Chronic pain is very amenable to complementary therapies such as guided imagery and hypnosis or biofeedback, movement therapies such as yoga and T'ai Chi, acupuncture, massage and craniosacral therapy.

I see June, a woman in her forties who had become disabled as a result of significant neck and shoulder pain for years that occurred following an injury, and eventually developed into fibromyalgia. She has seen several neurologists, orthopedists and pain specialists over the years, without much improvement, and was referred to our center by her pain management doctor to find out if any complementary therapies could be helpful. After six months of working with a combination of acupuncture, a special chiropractic technique called atlas-orthogonal technique, special exercises taught by an occupational therapist who also has extensive experience as a yoga teacher, and learning some self-care relaxation techniques, this woman has found significant relief from pain and now has hope for ongoing improvement as well as a better sense of her own ability to manage her pain and disability.

One of my patients, a psychologist named Raoul, had a heart attack several years ago. About three years after the event, he had a special heart test to look for any residual damage to his heart muscle. His cardiologist notified him that everything looked great, and in fact the evidence of prior muscle damage seemed to have totally resolved, which the cardiologist was at a loss to explain. Raoul explained it this way in a letter to his cardiologist, which he shared with me:

> *"In addition to several 'allopathic' practices, i.e. smoking cessation, reduction of fat in the diet, very moderate exercise, and daily atenolol* [a medication given to protect the heart after a heart attack], *there are other things I have been doing that I am certain have had a very important role in my recovery. I want to make you aware of these things because too often they are not*

stressed or even suggested as necessary or beneficial adjuncts to 'standard treatment.'

"One, that I consider most important, is psychotherapy...A heart attack is not just a physical event; it has emotional, psychological and spiritual meaning as well. It has a meaning about damage to the person's 'heart' – in all the meanings of that word. So, I have done a lot of emotional work and healing of my heart. My heart gave me a relatively gentle, but scary jolt to let me know about the need for work to be done on feeling past and unconscious heartbreaks. This work has enabled me to have more heart for myself...

"The second is Qi Gong, which is a physical exercise and meditative practice of drawing in chi energy (life force, positive energy, etc. whatever you want to call it) and using the chi energy to heal one's body. I did this practice once a day for most of last year...

"Last, but not least, is prayer. I have been on a prayer list...and have been prayed for every day for the last year. I also pray for myself occasionally, and I know other people pray for me as well. I've heard of much research...to substantiate the scientific validity of prayer, so I am including this as a possible reason for the healing as well.

"I hope this helps your understanding of my 'spontaneous recovery' or 'healing'. It certainly helps mine."

Raoul later spoke to the cardiologist on the phone and asked for his response to the letter. "His reply was kind of cynical" reported Raoul. "He said, 'A lot of people do these things and don't get better'." Raoul chose not to argue the point; he knows what he himself believes, and that is most important.

I had another patient several years ago who was diagnosed with advanced pancreatic cancer. There is really no good treatment at this time for pancreatic cancer, and this 41-year-old man opted to receive high dose vitamin C intravenously. There is some research on the anti-cancer properties of Vitamin C, and since there is not really a good conventional treatment for this type of cancer, I agreed to work with him. The average life expectancy after a diagnosis of pancreatic cancer is 3-6 months. This man lived nearly 2 years after his diagnosis, which he attributed to his high-dose Vitamin C therapy. Even the oncologists working with him were <u>very</u> surprised at his longevity with this serious condition, and even voiced the opinion that the high dose vitamin C must have been somehow quite helpful.

An older woman named Ann had longstanding back pain due to scoliosis, a mild curvature of the spine. She had seen several orthopedists, an osteopath, and used a heel lift in one shoe. After several sessions of acupuncture in our office without much relief, my Chinese medicine colleague suggested seeing our occupational therapist/yoga teacher for help with posture and exercises. This did the trick! Ann does her yoga stretching and exercise routine daily now and is pain free.

The list of successful cases could go on and on. But I can also describe cases where complementary therapy did not really seem to help. I had a patient with advanced breast cancer who refused all conventional surgery and chemotherapy or radiation. She insisted upon only using diet, crystals, and specially prepared water as her treatments. She did live for close to a year, but if she had received conventional treatment sooner, I am fairly sure her lifespan would have been longer. However, her treatment preferences were certainly hers to exercise, and she was adamantly opposed to any conventional treatment options that were recommended, clearly understanding the risk of an earlier mortality that she was taking. This was not a case of "integrative care" – using the best of all treatment modalities- but only "alternative" care, although her personal approach to her treatment was 'integrative' with her own values and beliefs.

I have had patients for whom acupuncture or homeopathy or nutritional interventions have not especially helped them. I have also had patients who have not experienced relief with conventional drugs and surgery. Each patient is unique. In my experience, the majority of people treated with the best of all available modalities have benefited. We need more research to evaluate all types of treatments, and come up with the most useful, least toxic options to offer our patients.

Social Results of Integrative Practices

What could be the societal implications of widespread inclusion of what are currently "CAM" practices into our mainstream medical practices and even everyday life? Suppose we taught children in school about the marvelous nature of their own mind-body. Imagine if we nurtured in those children ways to connect to their own innate healing power. Could it be possible that these children would grow up feeling very empowered, knowing that they had control over their body? Would they possibly decide to make different choices about what they did with their wonderful mind-body, such as not using harmful substances, smoking, or getting pregnant too young? Perhaps they would want to eat healthfully, exercise, manage stress and even prevent anger-related violence by using mind-body practices like meditation or deep breathing every day.

If more people learned internal controls for stress management – meditation, biofeedback, guided imagery – perhaps we would see less of the stress-related illness we now spend so much money treating with medication. Perhaps people would turn less to drugs and alcohol to self-treat anxiety, depression and stress by using their own inner stress management tools that they would have learned in school as children, and been encouraged to practice throughout their lives. Could such self-efficacy techniques be part of health promotion activities supported by insurance, churches, community service agencies, free clinics? What would our society be like if these values were pervasive in our health care and educational systems?

Self-management programs for chronic medical problems are proving to be very effective. The federal Agency for Health Care Research and Quality publishes a monthly newsletter about its funded research activities. As far back as April 1999 it reported on a self-management program for groups of patients with a variety of chronic conditions – arthritis, asthma, diabetes, heart disease, stroke, lung disease – whereby the group members helped one another make lifestyle choices and solve disease-related problems. The patients participating in these group education programs emphasizing self-management had fewer hospitalizations, fewer physician visits, decreased disability and health distress and increased social functioning. Better health outcomes, happier people and less cost! What could be more valuable for our ailing and expensive health care system than helping people with self-efficacy and self-management?

Innovative programs in juvenile detention centers have looked at the incidence of violent behavior when the diet is changed to a lower sugar, higher nutrient-rich diet. When Kool-Aid is replaced with water and fresh juice, the incidence of anti-social and violent interactions is significantly reduced. When alcoholics are given a nutrient rich supplement, their craving for alcohol declines dramatically. Biofeedback has had a similar beneficial effect on refractory alcoholic men studied in the Veteran's Administration health system. Jon Kabat-Zinn at the University of Massachusetts is studying the use of mindfulness meditation techniques in a prison population. The opportunities to help people become healthy and functional are potentially limitless, if we could alter our orientation from the "quick fix" of a pharmaceutical agent, and more toward helping people learn self-calming techniques. Could our world experience less hatred and violence? Could we have a greater chance at world peace? Very idealistic you are saying.... impractical, you are thinking. Perhaps. But the potential advantages are limitless. Can we start now?

True Science

We will have to have an open mind, however, about everything. Just because an intervention has no explanation, we cannot discard an empiric observation of effectiveness. And just because "we've always done it that way" doesn't mean it necessarily works. We may have to throw out some current mainstream practices that do not prove themselves to be effective. We tout the scientific method in medicine. We claim to be scientists. A true scientist *observes nature without bias*. So, we will have to observe those things with which we are not yet familiar, without the bias of our own mindset. Even though we cannot currently explain how therapeutic touch might be effective, we must accept the repeated observation that an individual using his or her own energy can influence the energy of another. Even though we have no framework to understand how homeopathy might work, we do have to accept the findings of properly conducted research that reports some effect is happening, separate from any observable placebo effect, in homeopathic treatment. We have to be aware of the so-called "Tomato Effect" when it comes to unconventional therapies.

Drs. James and Jean Goodwin wrote a now classic article that was published in the *Journal of the American Medical Association (JAMA)* in 1984 titled "The Tomato Effect: Rejection of Highly Efficacious Therapies." In it they discussed the fact that no one in North America would eat tomatoes until the 1800's because everyone was certain that tomatoes were poisonous. After all, they belonged to the "deadly nightshade" family of plants. Some nightshades do have fruit and leaves that can be highly toxic, such as belladonna and mandrake, which can cause death if ingested in sufficient amounts. The fact that the French and Italians were eating tomatoes in large quantities with no untoward effects did not sway the public in North America who were staunchly sure tomatoes were poisonous. Only when someone dared to eat a tomato on the steps of a courthouse in

Salem, NJ - and survived - did Americans begin to consume tomatoes.

In medicine, we often ignore or even summarily reject therapies we cannot explain, even in the face of scientific evidence of effectiveness. If something does not fit our prevailing understanding of physiology or pharmacologic effect, we tend to dismiss it. This is what has happened with homeopathy. There is no current theory of how homeopathy could possibly work that fits with our understanding of human physiology and the effect of external agents (i.e. drugs) on the human body. So it can't work, and therefore we do not even believe the research studies that show it sometimes does work. As the Goodwins point out in their article, we should always ask "is this a placebo?" before accepting a treatment, and also "is this a tomato?" before rejecting one.

As we expand our health care repertoire to include all modalities and techniques that prove useful, and change the payment system to offer choice plus individual responsibility, we can move closer to a medicine that is scientifically-based as well as humanistic and individually focused. A medicine we all want for our loved ones and ourselves.

CHAPTER 5

A HEALING HOSPITAL

A "healing hospital?" How and why is that such a novel concept? Aren't hospitals designed to be havens of healing for the sick? The word 'hospital' itself comes from the French word *hospitale,* or guest room. Sick and injured people are admitted to hospitals every hour of every day all across the country. Most of them emerge repaired or improved enough to return to the community. The purpose of a hospital is to provide the latest in diagnostic techniques, surgical procedures and medical treatments. It houses the most highly trained staff 24 hours a day, 7 days a week to meet these serious and life-threatening illnesses and injuries. The very existence of hospitals is predicated on the need for a specialized healing environment.

However, I discovered something interesting when I queried the medical literature database called Medline in 1998 to see what kind of articles had been published in the prior ten years about hospitals and healing. I asked for the search to include "healing" and "hospitals" anywhere in the paper, not necessarily in the title. My search brought forth zero articles in the peer-reviewed medical literature with these two words found in the same piece. I was shocked. However, upon reflection I realized that we speak of healing very little in busy, modern mainstream medicine, as discussed in Chapter 4. We are currently concerned – if not consumed – with cost-effectiveness, evidence-based practice, clinical guidelines, efficiency, and sometimes clinical research. "Healing" seems sort of an antiquated, sophomoric concern in our ultra-modern, ultra-technological, highly sub-specialized hospital environments. But it is something our patients are desperate to find.

One hopeful sign is that when I did a similar literature search in 2005, I was happy to find several citations that dealt with hospitals and healing architecture (primarily from European journals) and several articles about healing and humor, spirituality, and quiet time in the ICU – all from nursing journals. And in 2010 the search revealed over 50 additional articles in this area. At least there is a start of the concept of "healing" in the medical literature about hospitals!

Every time I speak to groups of health professionals who work in modern hospitals, they literally cheer at hearing the concept of the hospital becoming a truly healing environment. They, like our patients, feel that their work environment too often seems almost prison-like. There are usually too few staff members to accomplish all the necessary tasks. Often, there is no time for a meal break, or even a rest room break. The paperwork, usually referred to as "documentation," has become overwhelming. Much of what is done in hospitals today falls under the category of "loss prevention" activities, or protection from lawsuits. Nurses (and doctors) are warned not to hug or touch patients for fear of harassment allegations. Everything one does in any role in the hospital environment is highly scrutinized by higher-ups and payers – for error, for efficiency, for cost-effectiveness. Overall, I have no objection whatsoever to being careful and following proper procedures to provide proper care. It is just that so much of everyone's energy is directed at error-avoidance and is generated largely from a basis of fear, that true caring, and therefore the healing environment seems undermined by these well- intentioned but now overwhelming 'documentation' and legal requirements.

Inhospitable Hospitals

Hospitals in the United States today have become bastions of technology. This is not a bad thing at all – most of us want ready access to the latest medical technology if we, or our family ever need it. But few of us welcome the opportunity to go into a hospital, or can recall having had a particularly healing experience as a patient. More often, we experience an over-extended nursing staff, doctors who are trying to fit in their hospital rounds between other commitments, and utilization reviewers trying to be sure we are discharged as soon as possible.

And don't forget about the error rate in hospitals, and the 100,000 Lives Campaign (referenced in Chapter 2.) A hospital can be a dangerous place to spend time. Remember my patient Tina, who saw the need to take on an advocate role for her father during his hospital treatment for a stroke? Another patient of mine, Jari Holland Buck, wrote a book about this significant role a family member can perform as an advocate for their hospitalized loved one. With the gripping title of *24/7 or Dead*, Jari tells the story of her husband's prolonged hospitalization (in several different hospitals) and the critical role she played in literally keeping him alive. Her book (recently retitled *Hospital Stay Handbook*) offers practical advice for family members of a hospitalized person to help keep track of their safety, as life-endangering mistakes or omissions are unfortunately all too frequent in modern hospitals.

Few people actually touch us in a modern hospital. There is no such thing as a bedtime backrub to help us sleep better. And hospitals are generally noisy, hectic places where a lot is happening day and night, so we get little rest.

I was amazed, as I spent days and nights in the hospital with my mother while she was so ill, at how noisy the place is. The housekeepers bang trashcans around at midnight. After all, they're wide awake! Staff members' beepers and cell phones ring out constantly. Other patients in the room are crying or moaning all night. The machines beep and their alarms go off. There is virtually no privacy. A typical hospital is not a particularly healing, restful environment. And there are usually no comfortable accommodations for visiting family members.

Perhaps this is how things must be, especially in the planning rooms of bottom line-oriented organizations. But there is data now showing that taking more time to explain procedures to patients, touching them in a caring and therapeutic way, offering pre-operative and post-operative relaxation techniques like soothing music or self-hypnosis can all offer not only clinical benefits to patients, but perhaps even lower overall costs and shorter hospital stays.

Dr. Mehmet Oz, a cardiovascular surgeon at Columbia University (and now a famous TV doctor), has published data on shorter healing times and less use of pain medication in patients who have been prepared before heart surgery with guided imagery and relaxation techniques. Planetree, a non-profit consulting organization founded by an disgruntled hospital patient, has helped transform many hospitals around the country into healing environments, more oriented to patient needs, and often showing not only shorter hospital stays, but more satisfied staff.

A *Healing* Hospital?

What would a healing hospital be like? It would be a place that feels, from the moment one walks in the door, that actual healing is occurring here. The colors, lighting, sounds, furnishings and scale of the place would all be designed to be inviting, warm, and human. The physical space would be designed to optimize therapeutic energy. Some innovative architecture and planning firms are beginning to specialize in the design of more healing environments for health care. Often these designs include access to, or a least visual contact with nature in the form of gardens, water features, and trees. They take into account feng shui, or energetic flow of the environment – such as the award-winning Continuum Center for Health & Healing at Beth Israel Hospital.

More data is being gathered about the healing aspects of color, light, sound, furniture placement, and even aromas on our emotional state. And emotional state sets the background environment for healing to occur. A frazzled, frightened patient is in a much worse frame of mind to heal than is one who is calm, open to help from others, trusts the caregivers and feels safe.

The food in a healing hospital would be nutritious and simple, probably mostly whole foods for those patients who are able to eat. Andrew Weil has called "the abysmal food served in hospitals" a "national scandal." We all know stories of a friend or family member who receives a tray with fried chicken and gravy immediately following recovery from a heart attack. This scenario would not be considered healthy nutrition. The people who design menus and food plans would understand the medicinal aspects of various foods, and might use concepts from ancient Indian Ayurvedic medicine and other healing traditions to utilize the optimal tastes, temperatures, spices and types of food to help treat a particular patient's condition. Ayurvedic medicine, for example, matches the taste and qualities of a particular food to help balance deficiencies or excesses in a person's constitutional type, or "dosha." In this philosophical framework, various aspects of food can help a person's health improve.

The food would also be nutritious for visitors and staff members. Who decided that McDonald's or Burger King should have franchises inside hospital cafeterias? Such a poor health message to give in a healing place! The healing hospital would have no such options on site.

Each patient's room would have music available to match the medical needs of that person's condition. We are beginning to understand more and more about the therapeutic value of sound and rhythm, and even becoming better at finding the proper music therapy prescription to alleviate anxiety, promote recovery from surgery, enhance cardiac rhythmicity, and calm premature infants. For example, hearing music that has a rhythm of about 60 beats per minute can calm a patient experiencing anxiety or pain. This rhythm corresponds to the heart rate of a person in a relaxed state. We can use this information about the healing aspects of music to our patients' benefit in many situations.

What Would Happen in a Healing Hospital?

People with serious illness and injuries would receive treatments as they do currently. They would have surgery, undergo diagnostic studies, and benefit from available medical treatments just as they do now.

In addition, however, they would actively and consciously receive emotional, physical and spiritual support throughout their stay. "Integrative medicine" would truly be practiced there. Nurses would actually touch them – providing the old fashioned backrubs of yesteryear. Most nurses who have been around for a while will tell you that when patients experienced a nightly backrub in the hospital, they needed far fewer sleeping pills and anti-anxiety medications than they currently require. Most nurses would be trained in Therapeutic Touch, and utilize this energetic healing technique in appropriate situations. Therapeutic Touch is a method in which the practitioner utilizes his or her own sensitivity to the body's energy emissions to help soothe and "unruffle" the disturbed energy of the person being treated. There is a large body of research in the nursing literature that supports the effectiveness of this technique for a wide variety of health problems.

Massage therapists and body workers would be on staff to provide therapeutic massage for patients with various medical conditions. They would also be available to provide support and physical healing to staff members and patients' families. The staff in a healing hospital would also have access to stress reduction programs, such as mindfulness-based meditation and yoga. A study conducted at Lehigh Valley Hospital in Allentown, Pennsylvania showed that such a mindfulness-based stress reduction program lowered burnout and improved well-being among nurses in that system.

Patients in a healing hospital would be instructed in healing imagery and relaxation techniques prior to surgery, if they were able. Anesthesiologists and surgeons would be very cognizant of the healing power of their words and actions during general anesthesia, and would utilize this knowledge during anesthetic induction, throughout surgery and upon awakening the patient as well. Recovery room nurses would be facile in the use of imagery and relaxation techniques for use in the immediate post-operative period. Energy workers might even be in the operating room to provide healing energy for the patient, as well as for the doctors, nurses and technicians who work so hard to help the patient. Doctors, nurses and others would learn to practice their own "centering" activities before the operation starts, in order to maximize their own healing energies.

Healing imagery would also be used to help patients manage pain, nausea and other physical discomforts. Medication, of course, would be available, but would likely be needed in smaller amounts as the patient is enabled to use her own "inner natural pharmacy" as well.

If a person in the hospital is dying, all the healing aspects of leaving this world in a state of grace would be mobilized, as is now often done in hospice environments.

I once heard Michael Lerner, the director of Commonweal in California, speak about healing as the "movement toward wholeness that grows out of our wounds." Commonweal is a residential center for people with cancer to learn healing techniques to help them travel the journey of their disease, even if the journey is to the end of life. Dr. Lerner gave an example of an experience he had during a trip to India where he visited a small hospital. Each morning before starting work the hospital staff would gather and say a prayer together: "Dear Lord, above all things let us this day do no harm."

Dr. Lerner described those who do the most harm in health care are those who 1) have not mastered their technical skills; 2) have not developed wisdom; and 3) have not had any wounds themselves, so they do not empathize with the people they serve. In truth, we all have had wounds. We need to be aware of them, and use what we have learned from our own wounds to help others. We just need to be our own authentic selves in order to empathize with others and their pain and wounds.

Who Would Work in a Healing Hospital?

Certainly, all the types of health care professionals currently working in hospitals would be there: nurses, pharmacists, aides, x-ray technicians, respiratory therapists, physical therapists, dieticians and so forth. In addition, new kinds of practitioners, not generally utilized in allopathic hospitals, would be evaluated for skill and ethical practice and be given privileges to serve patients' needs as well. Healing practitioners like massage therapists, music therapists, art therapists, acupuncturists, energy workers, chiropractors, and others – all the kinds of therapies that show results in assisting sick people to get better would be incorporated into the staff of a healing hospital. Already many hospitals or special units such as oncology, psychiatry, rehabilitation or pediatrics have some of these types of practitioners on the staff. The healing hospital would have such persons and therapies available to anyone who might benefit from their care and expertise, just as they now have access to respiratory therapists, physical therapists, and other health care specialists.

Many conventional health care workers would love to work in this kind of hospital. To truly participate as a caring individual in the healing process of a sick person is the reason all of us went into a health profession in the first place. To actually be able to work in an environment where energy is directed at the healing process at all times in all ways would be very nurturing of our own energies as helpers to the patient. Few, if any of us, became doctors, nurses, or technicians in order to fill out endless forms and learn to follow "clinical pathways", "protocols" or "practice guidelines". We do not want to see our patients as nothing more than flimsy-gowned lumps of protoplasm gone awry. We want to help real, live human beings in need, and we want that help if we ever need it.

Work shifts for caring professionals would be limited to a reasonable amount of time. The 12-hour nursing shifts that have become the norm in hospitals today are not necessarily healthy for the worker nor for the patients they care for. Remember the Institute of Medicine's study on medication errors in hospitals (illuminated in Chapter 2?) According to research conducted by the federal Agency for Healthcare Research and Quality (AHRQ), factors that clearly contribute to more hospital errors are 1) the staffing shortage of nurses in hospitals and 2) the lengthy hours they work. Data from a study of nearly 400 nurses published in *Health Affairs* in 2004 showed that errors were 3 times more likely to occur when a nurse worked a shift longer than 12.5 hours. This information has prompted the Institute of Medicine to issue a recommendation prohibiting "nursing staff from providing patient care in any combination of scheduled shifts, mandatory overtime, or voluntary overtime in excess of 12 hours in any 24 hour period and in excess of 60 hours in a 7 day period." They further state that "No amount of training, motivation, or professionalism will allow a person to overcome the performance deficits associated with fatigue, sleep loss, and the sleepiness associated with circadian variations in alertness." This all seems like common sense, really.

Working hours of doctors, especially interns and residents have been under scrutiny and now regulation in the past few years. Many studies have documented the dangerous errors that occur with excessively long work hours of doctors in training. So much pressure has been laid to bear on the entities overseeing resident education requirements, that all specialties have implemented maximum resident work hours of no more than 80 hours in a week with at least 12 hours off after any 24-hour shift. This pressure was initiated after the daughter of a powerful New York politician died in the emergency room because of errors committed by an overly fatigued resident.

I certainly remember my days as an intern and resident in the late 1970's. Those 120-hour workweeks were not good for us, or for our patients.

A Better Standard of Care?

How would a healing hospital be better than our current standard hospital? Would it cost more, or less? Could it "heal" the organizational bottom line financially? I believe people would love to be helped in an environment that speaks 'healing' in every aspect. In today's competitive world, where every hospital is trying to outdo its competitors, happy, healed patients and family members would be a hospital's best recruiting and advertising source.

Health workers would stay rewarded and joyful in their work. They would become very loyal to their hospital. Staff turnover would be markedly reduced, and cost savings would result. Recruiting, training and retaining good employees are huge, expensive challenges for hospitals today. Some estimate that it costs approximately $60,000 to recruit and train a qualified nurse for a hospital. A happy, loyal workforce that loves to come to work is not only a joy, but an economic boon to the hospital as well.

There is growing research showing better patient outcomes when some of the healing techniques described above are employed. Surgical complications are lower and the need for pain medication is reduced when patients have pre- and post-operative relaxation training and support. Hospital stays are shortened, use of drugs is less, and therefore, again, costs are lowered.

Improved patient outcomes at lower cost and fewer days in the hospital would be very attractive for payers. Healing hospitals would enjoy a competitive advantage in the current competition for good insurance contracts.

Why Aren't All Hospitals 'Healing Hospitals?'

A healing hospital would be much more enjoyable and rewarding in which to work, receive care, and visit friends and relatives. It would be cost-effective and provide improved patient outcomes. So why isn't every hospital in America tooling up to become a healing hospital?

Some hospitals believe they are already doing this. They say they are a "patient- centered organization striving for excellence in care," or some such mission statement. I am sure they honestly believe they are. But find out if they allow energy healers on their staff to help manage pain, or if the surgeons routinely give intravenous vitamin C after surgery to improve wound healing. Generally, the conventional U.S. hospital administrator and chief of staff would reel at such thoughts. "Unscientific" they might say, or "too 'New Age' for us." Mostly hospitals (and American medicine in general) are very conservative. They are not really willing to stick their necks out and try something new, even if it would be of tremendous benefit to those they serve *and to themselves*. Remember the Tomato Effect (discussed in Chapter4)?

But, there are some examples of creative, paradigm-shifting organizations, willing to advance some innovative ideas. One example is the North Hawaii Community Hospital in Waimea, Hawaii. Earl Bakken, the founder of an important medical technology company, thought he was going to retire on the Big Island. Instead, he got recruited to help develop a community hospital for the residents of northwest Hawaii. His vision for the 50-bed hospital, which opened in 1996, was to offer the best in both high-tech and high-touch medicine and to heal the mind, body and spirit. It is the first hospital in the U.S., which combines conventional allopathic medicine and ancient Hawaiian, Asian and holistic healing approaches. In 1999, it was rated number one in the nation in patient satisfaction by Solution Point. North Hawaii Community Hospital dispenses pharmaceuticals and herbal medicines from its pharmacy. Its staff includes physicians in all specialties and also naturopaths, acupuncturists, chiropractors and massage therapists. Each hospital room opens to a garden and the sound of water is pervasive. Skylights bring sunshine into the lobby, hallways and operating rooms. Hawaiian art is everywhere.

Pacific Medical Center in San Francisco has long been a leader in incorporating complementary techniques into its therapeutic approach to patient care. It is part of the Planetree system of patient education facilities that give people access to health information to become better consumers of health care. It also sponsors an integrative medicine center on its campus.

Columbia University's cardiac surgery unit, under the direction of Dr. Mehmet Oz, is becoming renowned for its exploration into the use of mind-body practices to help patients undergoing open heart surgery recover more quickly, lose less blood in surgery, and utilize fewer hospital days.

Sutter Health Systems hospitals in California offer guided imagery before surgery. Queens Medical Center in Honolulu offers healing touch. Many children's hospitals in the country, including ours in Kansas City, offer integrative pain management programs with imagery, healing touch, acupuncture. Some programs are kept rather quiet, others widely advertised.

Beth Israel's Continuum Center for Health & Healing has been described above. The Greenhouse Project is a movement in the long-term care area that seeks to offer a homelike environment for elders who need full time care. The small facilities are actually like homes, with pets, children, gardens and other aspects of real life in a real community rather than the usual more sterile and malodorous nursing homes we are accustomed to today. Hospitals in the Spirit of Women network are working on introducing healthier food choices in their member hospitals. I heard Dr. Michael Roizin speak at my local hospital. (Dr. Roizin co-authored *You: the Owner's Manual*, *You: the Smart Patient* and *You on a Diet* with Dr. Oz.) He indicated that at his hospital, unhealthy food choices have been eliminated. There might be a McDonald's but they can't serve French fries!

Hospitals for a Healthy Environment is an organization of innovative health care centers that are sharing this vision of environmentally-conscious environments are also cost-effective. The Center for Health Design is a research and advocacy organization of innovative healthcare, architecture and design professionals leading the way to improve quality through consciously designing buildings that are healing environments. Early evaluation of buildings designed by this group for hospitals have shown these facilities to be superior to conventional hospitals in actually improving patient outcomes and the organization's bottom line.

More and more hospitals will bring into their units some or all of these ideas, and more. Many are waiting for research data to help direct their decisions. Some need money for physical plant renovations. Most are likely holding back until insurance will reimburse for therapeutic touch or acupuncture treatments. Hiring staff to perform activities that are not reimbursed is an undertaking most hospitals are not prepared to handle at this point.

But someday, this concept of the healing hospital will be the norm, and we will wonder why it took so long.

CHAPTER 6

A NEW KIND OF MEDICAL SCHOOL

Doctors of the future must be prepared for the new kind of practice being described in this book. They will be team partners in a much larger team, and work in environments unlike the ones we are used to today. This preparation will require some changes in the content of the medical school curriculum, in the way that curriculum is taught, and in the role modeling students observe during the educational process.

The curriculum must continue to be based on scientific reasoning, on data and evidence about mechanisms of disease and illness, in treatment efficacy, and in the ability to interpret the medical literature. These objective, rationalistic skills and methods must be balanced with the "art" portion of medical practice which emphasizes listening with empathy, expressing genuine caring toward the person and building a true partnership with patients. The concept of assisting the patient in his or her healing process through the expression of love is a crucial part of any healing system, and needs to be investigated, modeled and rewarded more openly in medical education.

Love and Medicine

I recall an experience I had while in my third year in medical school that challenged my innate sense of the importance of empathy and love in medicine. It was my first clinical rotation, where we finally got to move from the classroom and laboratory to nearly full time in the hospital and clinics to see patients ourselves under the supervision of residents and faculty. I was fulfilling my surgical rotation at a county hospital, and had been assigned two patients to evaluate and follow closely through their hospital stay. I was thrilled to finally be talking with a patient on my own, trying to remember all the questions we had been taught to ask, in the proper order, and writing up the history and examination findings in the chart. The actual one-on-one contact with the patients was the most exciting. I was finally feeling what it was like to be almost a doctor. I did find the operations fascinating, and received very good instruction from my teachers.

One evening, I had a pivotal experience. My patient was to go into surgery the next morning to have a diseased adrenal gland removed in order to manage her rare form of hypertension and she was very frightened. I had gone into her room to check on her that night and found her crying. I sat on the edge of her bed and took her hand to console her and let her express her fears for the upcoming surgery. She needed someone to talk to. She had no family, and not a single person had visited her during her hospital stay. The surgical team was very competent and thorough, but as the medical student, I was really the only one with time to spend talking with her.

My supervising resident passed the doorway to the room as I was sitting with the patient and touching her arm. When I came out to the nurses' station a few minutes later, he reprimanded me. "What were you doing in there?" He asked. "You are the doctor, not the social worker." When I told him how frightened she was contemplating major surgery all alone, and how she just needed a few minutes of human caring, reassurance and love, he laughed. "You won't have time to do THAT when you're a real doctor. That's not your job, anyway."

I learned quickly "my job" was to aspire to be the person with the authority and power. I was supposed to become the person with the medical (i.e. technical) skills who could not afford the time or the emotional cost of "getting involved" with the people who would be the beneficiaries of my superior abilities. The human aspects were to be left to other (in my resident's view "lesser") beings such as nurses and social workers.

I had serious doubts right then that maybe I was entering the wrong profession. I wanted to care about the people who would entrust their bodies, fears and secrets to me and the team of doctors in the operating room, emergency room or clinic. I wanted the vulnerable person to feel safe and cared about, as well as confident in our technical skill. After much soul searching and self-doubt, I decided that maybe I really was in the proper profession; I just had to keep my aspirations about humanism under wraps until I could be on my own later. I did decide to continue to talk with patients, hold their hand if necessary, and sit on the edge of their bed. Many years later as an "attending" – or teaching physician – myself, I developed a reputation for being the faculty member who hugged patients on rounds in the hospital and in the clinic. I role modeled what I felt was important, but missing from my own education so many years before. And I have received feedback from some of my former residents, even years later, that the hugs were one trait they always valued having learned from me.

I still hug my patients every day (after asking if they would like a hug; only rarely do they decline.) I read somewhere that humans need five hugs a day to stay healthy, and discovered early on that if I offered someone a hug and they accepted, I received one as well! I estimate getting approximately 10-20 hugs on a daily basis, and feel very healthy most of the time!

Sometimes what a person needs is not actually a physical hug, but some kind of emotional connection with the person from whom they are seeking help – a "virtual hug," you might call it! They want to be heard, taken seriously, and truly listened to. This helps us feel valued as people, and helps us realize that sometimes another person actually cares. For physicians and other health professionals, this is the key to a successful healing relationship. Sometimes it is referred to as "bedside manners."

Communication 101

I have frequently asked medical students to observe the responses of patients after being visited by various attending (or "teaching") physicians they work with through their educational program of medical school and residency. Sometimes the patient seems uplifted and hopeful about his or her condition or possibilities for healing; other times that patient's pain or depression is worse after the morning doctors' rounds. The attitude and connection a physician is able to create, even in a brief interaction with a person, can make a huge difference in the way that person physically and emotionally handles their illness.

My patient, Nancy, who is a 48 year-old mother of two boys started getting sick at about age 26 with Crohn's Disease, a serious inflammatory condition of the intestine. She also had been a nurse for many years both in hospital and office settings. But being a patient, she says, opened her eyes to a lot of things. She had functioned reasonably well until a few years ago when she developed a serious infection from a perforated colon. She had emergency surgery and was extremely ill. Her surgical wound broke open about a week after her surgery, and could not be closed with stitches – it had to heal from the inside out. This was a long and very painful process and she was in the hospital for 10 weeks. She met some absolutely wonderful nurses and doctors who she felt really cared about her and listened to her and did whatever they could to alleviate her suffering and give her encouragement. Some others were memorable in a negative way. She sometimes felt disrespected and degraded, and treated as a "side show" due to her large and unusual wound, as medical students and interns would come in to "gawk' at her embarrassing open abdominal wound. One time about 6 medical students came into her room and insisted upon listening to her lungs while she was using the bedside commode; they refused to wait just a few minutes until she was finished with a very personal task, in spite of her repeated pleas to "just give me a minute." She felt like an object with no humanity at all.

Nancy pondered her quagmire. She had to stay in the hospital to heal, but her soul was feeling way too stressed. She thought and thought and finally figured out a way to get the respect she deserved. She had her husband bring in a photo of her taken with her family a few months before she became ill, when the roots of her hair weren't gray, her hair was washed and brushed, she weighed 40 pounds less, had on makeup and was happy. The response was remarkable. The staff and medical students wondered "who is this pretty lady with a family in the photo?" She told them "It's me, it's really me." They began to treat her differently, as if she was a real person again, instead of "that loopy lady with the unbelievable wound." After this transition, she felt she had the energy and focus to really begin getting well, and things started looking up. How we doctors see people and treat them has everything to do with the healing process.

A former student, Lisa, is now a licensed physician, but remembers a heart-rending experience during her surgical rotation in medical school. The trauma team was caring for a patient in the intensive care unit who had literally lost the lower half of his body in an accident. Her attending surgery faculty member was called urgently to the bedside when the patient started to bleed profusely from his wounds. The surgeon was very excited and snapped orders to the nurses and students to bring needed items to him, including a special type of pressure dressing to stop the bleeding. After he stopped the bleeding and things had calmed down, while still at the bedside of this very frightened but alert patient he said "Well, there went $1,500." Then he rushed out of the room to get on to his next patient. Lisa stayed behind to offer some comfort to the traumatized patient who was visibly in pain and very scared by all the bleeding. She later was chastised for wasting time with a man who was clearly going to die anyway. Now she is also traumatized.

This story contrasts sharply to an experience I had during medical school with a dying patient, and has given me one of my most important lessons about caring for seriously ill and dying people. I was working in a rural hospital for a month, with a family doctor and the staff. We had a lady in the hospital dying of lung cancer. She had a tube in her trachea (a "tracheostomy") to help her breathe better. I was on duty along with a very experienced head nurse named Helen one Saturday afternoon, when the patient started coughing and bright red blood started oozing out the tracheostomy. I was quite alarmed and totally unsure what to do. I called for Helen, who calmly came in to the room, put on latex gloves, reached for some clean towels that were handy and put them over the tracheostomy. There was a suction machine in the room, and Helen coolly turned it on and started to suction the blood that was now literally pouring out of the women's throat. I was quite scared, as I had never experienced this sort of situation before. The entire time Helen spoke in a calm and reassuring voice, telling the patient that she was ok, that we were there with her, that she would not be alone as she passed away. Helen had seen plenty of people die, and was prepared for this woman's passing. She asked me to take the patient's hand and sit with her on the bed while she suctioned the blood. As Helen spoke, the patient, who had been panicky and agitated seeing all the blood, visibly relaxed. She smiled as best she could and thanked us. Slowly the blood drained out of her body, and she died. Her death was inevitable, and Helen taught me that a person who is dying needs to not be alone, and needs to be loved and supported through the dying process. When I die, I hope there are more Helens, and no one complaining about the cost of supplies they used to help me at my bedside.

Medical schools need to support, encourage and nurture such skills and sensitivities in our future doctors. Far from being "fluff," or "time-wasting," true expressions of caring from the doctor *are* an integral part of the physician's role, and most definitely assist the healing process. Ask any patient.

Curriculum Revisited

In terms of the "hard sciences" in the curriculum, the standard areas currently emphasized must continue to be cornerstones of what an aspiring doctor needs to learn: anatomy, physiology, microbiology, molecular biology, pharmacology, biochemistry and immunology. Biochemistry, however, needs to become much more relevant clinically.

Most schools teach biochemistry in a way that emphasizes rare diseases that are almost never encountered in clinical practice. What students are missing is an understanding of true clinical nutrition. How is energy made in the body, and why are vitamins, minerals and micronutrients so crucial for good health? We teach the complexities of the energy production cycle, but fail to discuss why nutrition plays such a crucial role in a person's complaints of fatigue, or pain, or sleep disorders. Most students graduate with little ability to actually talk with a patient about any meaningful details of their diet, and how to eat, or to consider supplements in certain situations of ill health or symptoms. While the average medical student receives 109 hours in biochemistry instruction, a 2009 survey published in *Academic Medicine* in September of 2010 (Adams et al) reported that students are exposed to less than 20 hours of required nutrition curriculum. Twelve medical schools (of 105 completing the survey) required 12 or fewer hours of nutrition instruction in the entire 4-year curriculum. So, the biochemistry curriculum needs substantial expansion and improvement, with a particular emphasis on clinical biochemistry – or what could be called 'human nutrition.'

In fact, medical students are asked each year upon graduation to evaluate their medical education by the Association of American Medical Colleges (AAMC.) In 2004, 51.8% of graduating medical school seniors believed their education in nutrition was "inadequate." 2004 was the last year this question was even asked.

MD's and Drugs

Pharmacology is an important part of the allopathic medical curriculum today. In fact, prescribing drugs is arguably the one thing MD's are trained to do best. The word "allopathy" actually means giving something "other" than or counter to the problem or symptom being treated. To compare other terminology, "homeopathy" means giving something like or similar to the problem being treated; "osteopathy" refers to using the bones or musculoskeletal system as the major therapeutic approach to managing illness.

To illustrate the "anti" nature of allopathic medicine, think about the names we have for our drugs: *anti*biotics, *anti*depressants, *anti*-hypertensives, *anti*cancer drugs, *anti*-virals, *anti*-diabetic agents. We have a pharmaceutical agent (or several) for any symptom or problem you can name. However, we do not teach much about the therapeutic aspects of botanical or plant products. The therapeutic effect of plants is a field called "pharmacognosy" – herbal medicine. While most physicians are unlikely to become herbalists, they at least need a working knowledge that this field exists, and which plants can be safely and effectively used therapeutically and which ones could be dangerous. Physicians and medical students express more and more interest today in learning about herbal medicine. In fact, many of our earliest pharmaceutical agents came from plants (for example the heart drug digitalis derives from foxglove; colchicine for gout comes from autumn crocus.) Some of our modern chemotherapeutic agents still come from the plant world – such as taxol, an anti-cancer drug from the yew tree. Using direct plant extracts has been practiced by nearly every culture for as long as humans have existed, and we need to study and learn more about them. We also need to have our future physicians become more knowledgeable about both therapeutic and toxic plants, drug-herb interactions, and herb-herb interactions. Our patients want us to know.

Medicine for Each Individual

A fascinating and effective whole-person approach to health care is a field called "functional medicine." This arena looks at the unique ecology of each individual in terms of that person's genetic predisposition for disease, environmental influences such as toxins, stressors, activity levels, emotional supports, intestinal flora, allergic tendencies, nutrient excesses and deficiencies, and then develops interventions specific to the person's unique biological setting and lifestyle practices. Nutritional expertise becomes crucial in helping the person achieve maximal function. We are seeing more and more chronic and degenerative diseases in our modern world – conditions brought on by poor lifestyle choices, environmental toxins, free radical damage (from ionizing radiation in the atmosphere, toxic buildup of oxidants from smoking and inflammation) and stress. Some examples of the chronic diseases or conditions that result from the above accumulation of cellular damage and imbalances include arthritis, depression, fibromyalgia, irritable bowel syndrome, chronic fatigue, obesity, diabetes, Alzheimer's disease to name some of the common ones.

Functional medicine attempts to address these problems in a comprehensive manner that shuns the labeling we tend to use in standard medicine (i.e. the "diagnosis"); to look deeper at the underlying cellular processes that are malfunctioning and work with the patient to enhance healthy nutrition and lifestyle choices, manage stress and address fundamental system imbalances. This approach contrasts rather sharply with our usual goal in medicine: to find the diagnosis, then move to the proper drug or surgery to treat the illness, rather than realizing that the end result – the disease or dysfunction – is occurring because of a complex web of interactions among all the aforementioned aspects of functioning, and usually cannot be "cured" by giving one or several pharmaceutical agents.

Dr. Halstead Holman called for an overhaul of medical education in this regard in his September 2004 article in the *Journal of the American Medical Association* entitled "Chronic Disease: the Need for a New Clinical Education." He discussed the way in which physicians are educated to look for the one unifying diagnosis and then the one or more treatments, usually drugs, to manage the disease. In chronic illness this model works poorly - there are many interdependent problems and dysfunctions that require a much more individualized approach, and often drugs can be more a problem than a solution.

This field of functional medicine will need to be a pillar of the curriculum in the new medical school, as it brings together all we know about the human organism - physiology, biochemistry, anatomy, pathology, immunology, pharmacology, endocrinology, human behavior, neurology, and so forth – to apply toward the healing of a complex human. It is medicine focused on the individual, using scientific knowledge to improve functioning and assist the body in its own magnificent self-healing abilities.

Using a functional medicine approach, we will be able to "compress morbidity" as James Fries, MD from Stanford medical school suggested in his 1980 article in the *New England Journal of Medicine.* We may not prolong the human lifespan, but with improved functioning of all our cells, we will spend less time being ill and dependent at the end of our lives, and therefore spend less time (and less money) on long term care in nursing homes and rehabilitation units. We will, ideally, function well until our body's lifespan is exhausted, and then have a very short period of illness and disability before dying. I think this is the kind of death most of us want for ourselves.

What about "Preventive Medicine?"

Prevention, while discussed a lot in medical circles, is really given short shrift in our educational process, in our payment system, and in our cultural norms. We do not especially encourage healthy lifestyles among our medical students, practicing doctors, nurses or anyone in the health care world. Students are stressed to study, study, study; memorize, memorize, memorize. Interns and residents are still required to be in the hospital for extended hours, with few breaks for nutritious food, rest or exercise. Often when a student decides to take an exercise or play break from their studies, they feel guilty. Residents have to "sneak" time to grab a meal on call. The "successful" resident or "bright star" student is still usually the one that sublimates his or her own human needs in order to excel academically. I am not criticizing the goal of academic excellence. I want the doctors who take care of me to be smart, knowledgeable, and serious about their profession and their heavy responsibilities and be very well trained. But I also want to be sure they are rested enough to make sound decisions, careful enough to write my prescriptions correctly, centered and calm enough to remove the correct body part, or make a life-saving decision in an emergency. Doctors need rest and nurturance in order to be able to do their job well; medical students need to see this modeled more often and given proper priority during the educational process.

An article in the September 15, 2010 *Journal of the American Medical Association* revealed that 53% of surveyed medical students had significant burnout. A significant percentage of these burned out students reported less altruistic values and more unprofessional conduct than students who were not burned out. This study seems to be a strong statement for the need to support doctors in training and help them deal with stress, so as to prevent burnout.

An incident that I will never forget occurred during my third year in medical school. It could be described as the antithesis of "support". My attending (supervising or teaching) physician, a young man who had just finished his own training at an eastern renowned medical center, asked me some questions one day on rounds about elevated cholesterol. Seeing that I was unversed in this area, he challenged me to give a short presentation the next day on this topic, a common teaching technique used in medical education, and often very effective, since it builds on a real patient problem being addressed by the team of doctors at the moment. My attending suggested several resources I could find in the library to help my search for information on this topic. I dutifully went to the library and looked up his suggested references, plus a few others, and came away quite confused actually. I tried to summarize what I learned so I could make a presentation the next morning on rounds. The next day he asked if I was ready, I said I would try to give the requested report. I did. He then said to the whole group of about 6 residents, interns and students. "Well, I purposely misdirected her to outdated literature, to see if she would have the intelligence to do her own research. I give you a D on this presentation. A person gets a C grade if they look at the current textbooks on a given topic. They get a B if they also look in some general review journals. I only give an A to a person who spends many hours researching all the most recent research articles." I wonder what he really expected us to learn? Not to trust our attending (teaching) physicians, because they really wanted to embarrass and intimidate us? I am sure he wanted us to learn to be independent thinkers, but his methods were mean-spirited. I know he was taught in this model, so it is all he knew how to do, but I consider this "teaching by intimidation" and has no real place in the education of doctors whose job is to help people heal. I was hoping this form of "education" was a relic of the distant past (I *am* that old!) But in a 2010 survey of graduating medical students conducted by the Association of American Medical Colleges (AAMC) 60% of students still reported occasionally or frequently being "publicly belittled or humiliated" by teaching physicians.

We certainly all want our doctors to be knowledgeable, curious and independent thinkers. But there are ways to model and teach that behavior that is not denigrating. The new medical school will use the supportive, not the intimidation model.

On a societal level, we have not really taken prevention seriously, either. Many insurance companies do not pay for "wellness" visits, and we doctors have to code the time we spend counseling patients about healthy living as some medical diagnosis that will be paid for. This lack of coverage for prevention is a big gripe among patients. Only as recently as January 2005 did Medicare actually start covering a one-time physical exam for new enrollees into the program. Other than that first visit, elderly people must pay 100% of the cost of any preventive medicine or wellness visits. And it was only a few years ago that Medicare began providing payment for screening mammograms, in spite of the fact that numerous other government agencies have long recommended screening mammograms for women of certain ages.

On a public health level we have also done poorly in supporting the activities and people that promote our health as a society. Public health clinics are sorely lacking in public funding to do their jobs well, to promote healthy living and even to protect us from public health threats such as widespread epidemics and bioterrorism. There has been a chasm in philosophy and education between medicine and public health, and in the medical school of the future, these two important fields will be better coordinated and their interactions more robust.

Smoking Cessation as an Example

One odd occurrence in today's world of preventive medicine is that insurance companies rarely cover the cost of behaviorally based smoking cessation programs, nor will they pay for a drug called bupropion if it is being prescribed to help a person stop smoking. They will cover that drug if the diagnosis is depression. On a regular basis, I have to fill out forms for a patient's insurance testifying that my prescription of bupropion (brand name is Wellbutrin ™) is for depression and NOT for smoking cessation. Why in the world would an insurance company **not** want to do anything reasonable to help their insureds quit smoking? It seems that this would save them money by avoiding the high costs that smokers ultimately incur in terms of health care costs, and help the patient become healthier. Seems penny-wise and pound-foolish, doesn't it?

Actually, I think we know why this scenario occurs. In today's terribly dysfunctional health care payment system, insurance Company A can be fairly certain that a given individual covered today by them will not be covered by that same company forever. By the time a smoker is likely to begin expending larger amounts of money on smoking-related illnesses, they will have changed insurance companies several times. So it is not in Company A's best interest to pay for smoking cessation today when they do not anticipate cost savings on that patient 10 or 20 years from now.

This could be another argument for a system in which everyone is placed into the same risk pool and all insurers must cover everyone: it is economically wise to spend money today to save it in the future, because all the insureds will still be in the same huge risk pool later also.

Another glaring example of prevention being bypassed for other priorities is the nearly total lack of physical activity and exercise carried out in our schools today. I remember being in elementary school in the early 1960's during President Kennedy's push to make Americans more fit and healthy. We had to perform various fitness activities and tests on a regular basis, and had one class period daily devoted to "physical education."

Today, with all the pressures on pubic schools to improve academic performance, there is virtually no physical education any more and we are experiencing an epidemic of obesity in our children that is truly frightening. A societal commitment to physical fitness as an important aspect of health is clearly in order. We know many chronic diseases can be **prevented** by keeping one's body weight normal, so making healthy lifestyle choices and optimizing physical fitness is a necessity if we are to control health care costs.

Stress Management and Illness Prevention

As we learn more about stress/distress and its effects on health and disease, we need to make stress management techniques a critically important part of the modalities all physicians know how to use. The science of psychoneuroimmunology needs to become a core part of the medical school curriculum, as it is the science of stress medicine.

Psychoneuroimmunology – or PNI – is the science of the mind-body connection. This is the field Norman Cousins began to bring to popular understanding in the 1960's and '70's with his book *Anatomy of an Illness*. PNI research has brought us information about the physiology of the stress response and how emotions alter brain neurochemicals which, in turn affect heart rate, blood pressure, pain modulation, intestinal activity, immune responses, sleep, energy – so many crucial aspects of human functioning. The fact that many medical students today know very little about this basic arena of medicine is, to me, highly negligent on the part of our medical education establishment.

A medical education experience brought home to me very poignantly the disservice we are performing today in terms of this educational deficiency about PNI. At the University of Kansas we started an elective for senior medical students in "Unconventional Medicine" in 1998. One activity we asked the students to work on during the four week elective was to develop and practice some sort of personal balancing activity. This activity could be yoga, meditation, journaling, art therapy, T'ai Chi – anything that they could do on a regular basis to find their own peaceful state and develop personal comfort with their own mind-body connection. Our hope was that they would then use such techniques themselves throughout the rest of their training and practice, and also perhaps help their future patients learn and practice such techniques. When we started the course, we were not sure that the students would actually do this part (since we gave it only a 5% weight in the course grade.) What was astounding to my colleague, Dr. Jeanne Drisko and me was that nearly every student commented on the written course evaluation that this activity was one of the most important experiences of the course.

One student's comments were particularly moving. This young man was completing his last month of medical school, about to graduate. He chose biofeedback as his technique, and discovered something incredibly important about himself and his future as a physician: "I truly did not realize the power of the mind-body connection until I started to do biofeedback. I discovered that my jaw muscles were tight most of the time, and I was not aware of it. I was able to learn to relax them with biofeedback. I see now that the mind-body connection can be so important a tool for me to use with my future patients, and for myself. Thank you for this opportunity to learn perhaps the most important part of medicine."

Every time I remember this incident, tears come. First, I am moved by the sincerity of discovery on this student's part. I am deeply grateful we were able to give him an opportunity to develop an important sensibility that will help him throughout his life and professional career. But I also become teary-eyed in sadness that this is a typical student in a U.S. medical school, who has had no exposure to this potent and valuable area of medicine. I am sad that we are graduating scores of medical doctors who have no appreciation for the power of the mind-body connection, and how it can be used to minimize and eliminate suffering and illness, and optimize well being. Psychoneuroimmunology in all its theoretical and scientific glory and in its practical usefulness must become a basic science in the medical school of the future.

Energy Medicine

A fascinating field that is difficult to discuss in conventional medical circles, but one with enormous power for healing, is the arena of energy medicine. It is a problematic area to discuss, because the observed phenomenon of energetic healing does not fit with our mainstream model of human anatomy, physiology, or pathology. We have no clear, objective way to "see" energy or its effects on humans yet. We certainly measure various types of "energy" everyday: electrical impulses in EKG's or heart tracings, electroencephalograms (EEG's), electromyograms (EMG's) and nerve conduction studies. We measure magnetic energy in various tissues when we perform an MRI. We do feel heat energy in and around the body when there is inflammation. But we cannot "see" the energy field around a person, except using special kinds of photography such as the Kirlian technique. Some sensitive people claim to be able to actually see the energy aura around a person, animal or other living object. Often these claims are somewhat suspect to the average physician-scientist. Because the observation is not one that is shared by the majority, it seems to be "weird" or "out there."

However, most all of us refer to the notion of a person's good or bad "vibes', or the feeling that we have in certain places that the energy just isn't comfortable. We intuitively know there is something a bit 'off' but may not be able to clearly articulate it. We all have also had the experience of feeling better physically and emotionally in the presence of some people, and worse in the presence of others. It is possible to be trained to actually sense changes in a person's energetic field, and practice some techniques to "smooth" that field or "balance" or "unruffle" it. These are techniques practiced by individuals trained in Therapeutic Touch, Reiki, craniosacral therapy, many kinds of massage techniques, ancient Chinese practices such as Qi gong, Native American healing and other types of energy healing. Actually, all humans are capable of sensing and using energy healing techniques, but our modern western culture does not yet embrace these.

When we eventually develop techniques to objectively "see" and measure these energy aspects of our beings, and objectively observe the effects of energy healing methods, we will move medicine into a new era. We are in a period now I like to compare to our state of knowledge before we had a bacterial theory of disease. Some physicians in the mid-19th century empirically noticed that dipping their hands in a chlorinated lime solution between autopsies and delivering babies resulted in fewer maternal deaths from "puerperal fever" – the fever of childbirth. Dr. Ignaz Phillipp Semmelweiss declared that physicians must be carrying some kind of 'humor' from the dead person in the autopsy suite to the pregnant mother in the delivery suite, and they should use the chlorinated lime to remove this humor.

He didn't know about bacteria yet, but he scientifically observed that the outcome was different if he cleaned his hands. One irony of this story is that the microscope, eventually used to see bacteria, had been invented by Laennec in the 1600's! But no one knew where or how to look for these microbes until nearly

200 years later. At the time, Semmelweiss was forced out of the medical society as a heretic and a quack. His views did not conform to the prevailing majority, and challenged the reigning world view. His expulsion exemplified very dramatically the Tomato Effect in medicine: an effective technique is rejected because it goes against prevailing theory.

He died in an insane asylum in 1865.

The second irony about Semmelweiss is that in the very same year he died, Joseph Lister introduced antisepsis into surgery. Lister's work was based on the microbial theory of disease that Louis Pasteur had just proven in sheep. Finally Semmelweiss was vindicated, unfortunately after his tragic death.

We have a somewhat parallel situation now with respect to energy healing. We have many empiric observations of the effectiveness of energy healing, especially research published in rather esoteric molecular and cellular biology journals and in the nursing literature, but we have no "energyscope" to use in order to measure this healing energy. Our prevailing model regarding health and illness needs to include an energy aspect. We do not have a readily available method that we believe in to see and measure energy. When we do, though, our understanding of health and illness and our ability to help the healing process through the proper use of energy techniques will move forward dramatically. We will probably enter a new era in medicine once again. And energy medicine will become a basic science in the medical school of the future.

Expanding the Health Care Team

We also need to give allopathic medical students a view of what non-allopaths know and do, so that our future medical doctors can be more aware of the modalities their patients may be using, and more open to widening the circle of the health care team. If we want true healing environments and healing opportunities for everyone, the conventional physician will need to be comfortable working with a wide variety of non-MD healers for the benefit of patients. The concept of "integrative medicine" is gaining momentum. More medical schools are beginning to offer electives in this field. In 2005, 64 of the 127 MD medical schools in the US had elective courses in complementary/alternative medicine. In a 2009 survey many schools had courses in integrative medicine, some had multiple lectures and electives, but none has a required course. In the 2010 AAMC graduation survey, one-third of graduating medical school seniors indicated their education in CAM was "inadequate."

Andrew Weil at the University of Arizona has started the first model of a formal training program for graduate physicians in integrative medicine, with a stated goal of training individuals who would start more integrative medicine training programs around the country. The University of Arizona is also coordinating a pilot project of incorporating integrative medicine training into the 3-year family medicine residency in eight programs around the country. Several other residency programs are offering a fourth year fellowship in integrative medicine.

More centers offering the combined services of a variety of practitioners are being developed, as we are beginning to experiment with the integrative concept. At last, physicians will not need to feel they have to have all the answers. Help is available!!

We also will want to teach and model excellent leadership skills to the doctors of the future. They will be working on and often leading very diverse teams of health care workers, and will need to have a high Emotional Intelligence, as Daniel Goleman describes in his books of the same title, as well as a good IQ.

Medical Schools as "Therapeutic Organizations"

If medical schools are to revise their curricula and train the doctors of the future who will practice in new kinds of clinical environments, using not only new technologies, but interface with new teams of healers, the medical schools might also need to change. Their research mission, which have been the driving force for most academic health centers in the US must remain vibrant and strong, but perhaps may need to be subordinate to the clinical mission of educating physicians who will care for patients.

Roger Bulger, former head of the Association of Academic Health Centers in Washington, DC wrote a wonderful editorial in *JAMA* in May 2000 titled "The Quest for the Therapeutic Organization." In this paper he discusses the major challenge to academic medical centers at the start of the new millennium not as the financial crisis medical schools are facing, nor the organizational crisis, nor the research mission, nor the opportunities offered by new technologies. He says the greatest challenge for the medical academic community is "to restore the marriage between humanistic concerns and scientific and technical excellence in health care delivery practices." He promotes the inclusion of patients on medical admissions and curriculum committees, research committees, and hospital committees seeking to determine or assess benchmarks of quality. His emphasis on putting the patient first in every decision the academic community makes would breathe new life into our medical schools, and make them the right environment in which to educate the doctors of the future.

CHAPTER 7

THE ROADMAP TO CHANGE: HOW DO WE GET THERE?

So, what is the overall vision of an improved health care system that I am proposing?

It would be one in which the patients are viewed as individuals with autonomy and responsibility, and specific needs for evaluation and treatment, having unique personalities, families, histories, genetics, lifestyles, belief systems and healing responses.

It is one in which healing environments – ambulatory centers, hospitals, long term care facilities, hospices – have all been designed specifically to enhance healing. The food is healthy, the air, views, sounds, aromas all contribute to the healing process. The workers in these centers are respected and nurtured, so that they can do the difficult work of helping the sick. We might even have entirely new types of facilities that include a medical clinic that focuses on functional assessment and management using a broad team approach, that focuses on integrating the best of all treatment modalities and offers help not only with medical problems using a multidisciplinary team approach, but also emotional and even spiritual issues, such as the meaning one finds in one's life. It could include a spa, an excellent restaurant serving delicious healthy food, retail space that offers useful products and literature for healthy self-care, exercise space, classrooms in which to learn self-healing techniques such as yoga, meditation, T'ai Chi, healthy cooking, and so forth. Maybe these facilities would be part of a larger campus that also houses an inpatient area for the sicker people, and perhaps even an area for long term care of the disabled or elderly that does not isolate them from the rest of the community.

Systems and settings of care in the future embrace and include all healing options that prove to be effective, and the health care team expands to include other practices and practitioners currently considered "alternative" or "complementary" - provided an appropriate basis in science supports their work.

Doctors in this new system will have been educated in a way that builds upon our current model of medical education to include understanding the importance of the mind-body-spirit connection, the fundamental cellular imbalances that can occur and how to approach re-balancing them safely and effectively. Doctors would be taught and encouraged to follow a healthy lifestyle themselves, and to be effective members of an expanded team of healing professionals. Love as an important aspect of the healing process would be an everyday expectation.

End of life care would be loving and humanistic, and we would be more comfortable as health care providers and patients in dealing with the transition from "cure" to "care." We would have social clarity about what we can afford to do and under what circumstances, and have fairness that offers proper care to all our citizens.

As for paying for this futuristic vision, the concept of insurance may still be viable, but it will have to be re-thought. Either we need to have a universal single pool so that risk is shared across a broad spectrum, or multiple insurers, each of which is prohibited from excluding people who have illness, pre-existing conditions or other risky attributes. This is the only way to make "insurance" actually work. *All people in our country would be covered.*

Furthermore, the insurance product needs to be totally portable. A high-deductible, catastrophic plan is reasonable, with mechanisms such as the Medical Savings Account (MSA) or Health Savings Account (HSA) to assist with the deductible portion. Workers or their employers could pay into the MSA/HSA and the insured would have choices on providers and types of care on which they spent their deductible. Eligible low income, disabled, or unemployed individuals could have government-funded vouchers to cover authorized care for the deductible amounts, and a government subsidy for the catastrophic care portion. As a society, we would openly discuss and debate services that would be covered with public funds, as well as those that insurers would be required to cover. In this way, we would have ethical rationing that is openly debated and understood by all participants in the system.

Insurers would provide incentives for healthy behaviors. Disease prevention and health promotion would be key aspects of health care in the future ideal system. We would promote health and self-care at all opportunities, and have fewer costs in the last years of life as we are able to "compress morbidity" through supporting function at every opportunity.

A "Pollyanna" View?

The preceding chapters have been very idealistic. "Sure, maybe one person can change the way they practice, but I can't do that," you may be thinking. "Maybe you can choose to earn less money, but I can't do that." "Maybe you are comfortable working on the fringe, but I couldn't do that." At first glance this book may seem really impractical: some pie-in-the-sky vision that cannot be implemented. "We're just victims. Nothing can be done." Or "if anything can be done, it's certainly not up to me."

Maybe it's too frightening to think each of us could really change. It would require courage and living with some fear, a very uncomfortable state. People often believe that the courageous are not afraid. But actually, as Eleanor Roosevelt observed: "Courage is not the absence of fear; it is taking action in the face of fear." Maybe what we need is the willingness to take difficult action, even if we are afraid - because the outcome of action might be so much better than the dysfunctional status quo.

If you agree to at least look at the possibility that the only real way to generate the change that we want is to first change ourselves, here are some thoughts on how we can achieve a health care system that 1) is more equitable, 2) is more accessible, 3) is more respectful of individual autonomy, 4) requires more individual responsibility, 5) offers the rebirth of the humanism we all want to see, and even perhaps 6) is more affordable.

Another observation from Gandhi in this regard seems appropriate:

> "Individual liberty and interdependence are both essential for life in society."

1.   What can doctors do?

We doctors could start by revisiting the reason we decided to enter medicine in the first place. What is our true purpose in life? Is it to serve others? Perhaps we wanted to have the feeling of contributing something to society? To feel a human connection to people in need, and use some of our own intelligence, experience and heart to help another soul who is hurting or in need? Is our true purpose to make a lot of money? Is it to have a very comfortable life, or prestige? Perhaps there are elements of all the above in our original goals to pursue medicine. But we should be clear about our goals and mission, and align our activities to support those goals.

We might also re-examine the definition of a profession, and compare that definition to what is happening to many of us in health care today. A professional, according to Webster's, is "characterized or conforming to the technical and ethical standards of a profession." A profession is defined as "a calling requiring specialized knowledge and often long and intensive academic preparation." The verb "to profess" has often been used in the sense of "taking the vows of a religious community or order." In a more secular context it means to "declare or admit openly or freely" the principles and ethics of a given field of practice. So many of my colleagues in medicine feel out of sorts in the conflict that arises out of being employed by an organization whose financial goals collide with the ethical vows we take as physicians. Our time honored Hippocratic Oath asks us to promise that we will help all and harm no one intentionally. It asks us to teach others and revere our teachers.

Yet many of the managed care systems that we work in ask us to prescribe drugs that are less effective, because they are less expensive. Or to deny certain types of care because it is not economically in the interest of the company. Or not to have medical students work with us in the office, because they slow us down too much.

As professionals, we may have to say **no** to some of these perhaps well-meaning but misguided directives from managers. They are not our professional superiors, even though they may be our employers. To remain true to our calling, our ethic, our profession, we may have to reject being employed by organizations that do not honor our professionalism. If we remain in compromised situations in spite of our inner knowing that it is wrong, we have no one to blame for our loss of professionalism but ourselves. We must make our practice choices based on our values if we are to change the system that we do not like.

We could join organizations like the newly created National Physicians Alliance, a small group of idealistic doctors who want to return to the core values of our profession: service, integrity and advocacy. This group's mission includes a dedication to improving health and well being and to ensure affordable, high quality health care for all people. Or another organization such as Physicians for a National Health Plan that has long advocated universal access to health care, and has a plan for accomplishing this.

Organizational Insiders

Many of us will choose to work inside organizations and affect needed change so we can function in concert with our own values. Many systems are responsive, and have the same goals as physicians and other health professionals. We need to support those systems and organizations, and help make them even better.

We may need to refuse to participate in health plans that usurp the decision-making control from the doctor and the patient. Some groups of physicians around the country have been doing just that, and finding there is actually power in ethical behavior as well as in numbers. More and more articles in the popular press as well as medical news sources are reporting on doctors who are taking cash only and not participating in any insurance programs. Some examples of these practices are SimpleCare in Seattle, or Dr. Peggy Mahoney in San Jose, California. These practices accept payment in cash at the time of service, and do not bill insurance companies. Office overhead is much lower, as there is no billing operation. Cash flow is good and patients become the doctor's employer. Some practices even charge by the minute, with signs posted in their waiting rooms with the fee schedule, like Dr. Lisa Grigg in Wallingford, Vermont. These doctors and others believe they are able to offer better and more personal service, less crowded waiting rooms, a shorter wait for service, office staff who know the patient - all without the administrative overhead of elaborate and complicated billing procedures and excess personnel.

This non-insurance model of practice is also how we operate at the Sastun Center of Integrative Health Care in the Kansas City area. We charge people at the time of service and give them paperwork to submit to their insurance company for reimbursement. We have no billing staff, no excess overhead for this extra work, and our patients are happy. We have a 95% or better collection rate, and good cash flow. Patients see their bill at the time of service and can ask questions or get clarification of any item they do not understand right on the spot, at the time of service. They can decide right then if these charges are worth the service they received. The only time we send a bill is when there are extensive email or phone consultations, or lengthy forms or letters that need to be taken care of, without a physical visit by the patient.

It is important to understand why it is that physicians joined managed care organizations and in signed up to be employed within corporations in large numbers in the last 20 years. An article published in the April 1999 issue of *The American Journal of Managed Care* reported on a survey of 210 primary care physicians throughout the U.S. that "the overwhelming reason primary care physicians affiliated with an HMO was to retain patients...to avoid a perceived penalty associated with lack of affiliation, rather than for positive reasons." This survey also indicated that physicians join HMOs and other managed care organizations also for "quality of life" reasons: more predictable work hours, more personal time, less administrative burdens. Many doctors seem to be involved with these groups largely out of fear, not because these systems are perceived as better for patients.

We also need to become much better versed in the costs of health care: our own charges, the costs of medications, tests, surgeries and other procedures. Many doctors are less knowledgeable about the actual costs of health care than are their patients.

Partnering with Patients

Another approach physicians can take is to become true partners with their patients, not with managed care companies, drug companies or corporations. With the advent of the Internet and virtually instant access to the entire universe of medical information, the public now needs someone who can interpret all this data and help them sort through what might be relevant to their situation. No longer is the physician the one with the information. Now everyone has it! But not everyone knows what that medical information means, or how to apply a career of clinical experience to arrive at an appropriate course of action in a given individual's case. Now is the time for physicians to be co-participants with patients, and become comfortable in that role.

We may need to look at the relationships we have with special interests, like drug companies or equipment manufacturers. Do we really need that free dinner that will tell us all about the latest (possibly unnecessary) antibiotic or allergy medicine? Can we not buy our own pens and scratch pads? Do we really want various logos of corporate interests floating around our offices? A free clock that says the name of a drug? Posters and clipboards and pens and coffee cups everywhere with different pharmaceutical logos? What does this tell our patients? That we are so impoverished, we need these freebies? Does it tell them these corporate interests, perhaps, unduly influence us? Are we so blinded ourselves that we do not even notice these clutter-producing items? Dr. Jerome Kassirer's 2005 book *On the Take* is an eye-opening must-read review of the undue influence of the pharmaceutical industry on American medicine.

We can take the lead of internist Dr. Bob Goodman who started an advocacy organization called No Free Lunch. Its logo is the international symbol for "no": a diagonal red line across the words "free lunch." His group's tag line printed on lapel buttons is "Just Say No to Drug Reps" and about 500 doctors have so far taken the No Free Lunch Pledge, vowing not to accept any industry gifts, money or hospitality.

Examples also abound about doctors who have taken on the insurance companies who deny needed care to patients. These are instances again of partnering with the patient, rather than the payer. One episode reported in an article titled "Rebels in White Coats" published in the May-June 2000 issue of the *Utne Reader* made me stand up and cheer: when hospitalization of a psychotic patient was denied, a psychiatrist told the reviewer, "I'm going to put her in a car and send her over to you." The claim was approved.

"Free" Samples

What about free drug samples? "Oh – I give these to my patients who can't afford their medication," the doctors say. When was the last time a doctor had a free sample of a cheap generic drug? Never. Sampled drugs are always the latest generation, "me-too" – or copycat - medications that are always more expensive and often no more effective than other drugs at our disposal. If none of us had sample closets, and instead pushed for legislation to lower drug costs and/or offer better pharmaceutical coverage for patients, samples would be unnecessary. Are we just developing Band-Aid approaches, like free drug samples, to compensate in minimal ways for the really big problems that exist in the health care system like exorbitant drug costs and lack of proper coverage?

Many leaders in healthcare and in academic medicine have called for a prohibition of free drug samples to physicians, and ask that the pharmaceutical companies instead give vouchers so low income patients can afford their needed medicines. A January 2006 article in *JAMA* outlined this aspect of "Health Industry Practices That Create Conflicts of Interest." Drug samples, they say, "provide a powerful inducement for physicians and patients to rely on medications that are more expensive, but not more effective. Samples also provide company representatives with access to physicians." I made a decision when I opened my practice not to see drug reps in my office or to have any drug samples at all. Occasionally a patient will request a sample from me, but I explain why I have none, and we perhaps agree on a small prescription of a medication to see how they respond to it.

Pharmaceutical companies sometimes also have access to the hospital committees that oversee the hospital's formulary, or list of drugs they will keep on hand for dispensing to patients when ordered by the physician. Hospitals do not buy and inventory every possible drug, they make decisions on which specific drugs in a certain class they will use, most often based on the best available evidence of effectiveness combined with cost. The authors of the JAMA article also call for an exclusion from these committees of any physician (or other health professional) who has any financial links to a drug company through contracts, grants or receiving any gifts from them.

Learn About Other Healing Methods

Currently in medicine, I see most of my colleagues pursuing treatments primarily with prescription medications. This is largely how we have been taught – first to determine the diagnosis, and then the proper treatment, which is usually a prescription for a drug. We are beginning to see that many useful therapies to help people are not within our pharmacologic tool kit: herbs, nutrients, mind-body practices, body therapies, acupuncture and many techniques patients can learn and use themselves with no doctor involved at all! We need to become familiar with some of these "complementary" techniques that we did not learn about in medical school, so our patients have the best of all options for healing available to them.

Understand and Confront Limits

Finally, we doctors need to become more comfortable with limits in health care, and especially the ultimate limit – death. Throughout our training, we are imbued with the sense that death is our enemy at all costs. We have not learned very well the balance of applying all possibly useful techniques to save life when the goal of functional living is possible, but then to help people have a good death when that eventuality is inevitable.

As Michael Lerner of Commonweal and others have asked, we need to question whether technologies are going to be our servant or our master. Our difficulty is usually in knowing when the line has been crossed between hope for ongoing useful life and no hope for life, but hope for a dignified, pain-free and "healing" death. We need more attention paid to that interface. We need to have the skills and emotional preparedness to help patients and families, and ourselves, face the end of life.

2.   What can other health professionals do?

Nurses and other hospital employees can seriously look at their work hours. Is it really in anyone's best interest to be working at a critically important job like nursing a sick patient in a hospital for 12 hours straight? No, it's just a better lifestyle to only work three days a week for 12 hours, than four or five days a week for 8 hours. Does that fit with a personal mission of healing the sick?

Hospital administrators and system managers can look at the health insurance contracts they sign and ask if these truly will cover the costs of providing good care. Every hospital seems so concerned about "market share" and not missing out on any "covered lives" that they often are willing to negotiate rates that force them to lay off nurses and other crucial staff, or offer horrible, cheap food, or otherwise compromise care. If all hospitals really could be honest and ethical about contracts that must cover needed costs, then the payers (insurance companies) would have to come through, or they would have no hospitals to offer their insureds and no one would pur

Hospital administrators and boards of directors can begin planning for hospitals that are truly healing spaces. The physical facilities will need some change to fit with the research described in Chapter 5, and new kinds of healing professionals will need to be sought and credentialed. A philosophy that completely promotes healing in all its aspects can begin now, and will prove to be the best thing you ever did!

3.   _What can patients do?_ (And remember, we are all patients.)

If we want more personal selection in health care, and more ability to use techniques and practitioners of our choice, we need to ask employers for benefits that provide this choice and autonomy. We may seek employers who provide more options in health plans, or who pay into a health savings account for their employees. If we work in a large organization, we may be able to work with committees of employees to help select options that we want. For those who are self employed, or must find insurance outside of a large employer's umbrella, look for a plan that offers discounts for healthy behaviors such as being a non-smoker, wearing seatbelts, or maintaining ideal body weight. Investigate whether a Health Savings Account with a high deductible insurance plan is right for you.

Live Healthier

One way to lower the cost of premiums and therefore the cost to employers is to practice more healthy living. If we are sick less and utilize fewer health services, the costs of health care decrease. We may have to change some of our own health behaviors – such as quitting smoking, getting more exercise, eating more healthfully, and learning stress management techniques that we actually spend time practicing (such as meditation, yoga, T'ai Chi, etc.) We need to realize that many illnesses are self-limited, and if we rest more, drink fluids and take over-the-counter remedies – including herbs and nutrients – we may not need to see the doctor or go to the clinic at all.

We can be honest with ourselves about our being overweight, or our lack of stress management skills. Let's face head-on other self-defeating health behaviors and decide to really begin to take care of ourselves. No pill can do this. It takes our own desire to be healthy and our commitment and love for ourselves to do the job.

As we become more informed consumers, we understand the costs and benefits of various tests and interventions. We need to ask questions about effectiveness and costs of recommended tests and treatments. We need to care about the relative costs of various providers and the quality of services we receive from them. We may need to budget for routine health costs, and use insurance for the unexpected, expensive events that we cannot predict.

Become Political (or at Least Vote!)

Electing public officials who really care about reforming health care is something we all can do. We need to look to true leaders who put the welfare of the public above the interests of corporate entities or their own political aspirations. So much energy has been spent in recent campaigns for public office criticizing the "other side" when perhaps together, all the political parties could unite to design a system that includes coverage for everyone, with appropriate choice, autonomy and responsibility by everyone. We shouldn't have to spend time, money and energy lobbying to get lower cost drugs from Canada. We should elect public officials who will put the interests of the public above the interests of the pharmaceutical industry, and force drug costs to be reasonable here in America.

We can work with local school boards (or even run for such positions) to remove non-nutritious foods from school cafeterias and vending machines, and promote healthy food choices from kindergarten through high school. We can urge school boards to include more time for physical activity, and maybe even reinstitute an emphasis on physical fitness.

Be Proactive

We can call the drug company 800 numbers that appear on their TV ads to complain about costly direct-to-consumer advertising that ratchets up the cost of drugs and provides no real public service. We can, as my husband frequently does, stop a pharmaceutical detail person in the elevator of your doctor's medical building to let them know the public is angry about the cost of drugs and direct-to-consumer advertising and huge pharmaceutical company profits at the expense of people's needs, asking them to perhaps relay to their regional manager that the pharmaceutical industry could improve its image tremendously by using its enormous wealth and political clout to work toward a real improvement in health care. (Sometimes my husband actually gets a civil response; more often a rapid-fire defense of "research costs", and occasionally a completely cold shoulder.)

Accept Limits

As patients, we have to come to terms with the reality that every possible technology may not be available to us. There are limits to what can be afforded by us as individuals and as a society. Who decides what we can have and not have is the difficult question. Currently, it is often the payer who decides that a given procedure or drug is not available to us. Perhaps it should be _we_ who decide, based on what we have chosen for insurance coverage, how much of our own resources we are willing to spend, evidence of effectiveness of the proposed treatment, and other factors that we use when deciding on any other expenditure we make in our lives.

Finally, we must face the fact that death is inevitable. Death and dying are topics we do not discuss freely in our society. Understanding and accepting death with grace may be one of the last frontiers of our medical and cultural development in the next century. Perhaps we can find guidance from other cultures that seem to realize that every day of life is a step closer to death, not in a morbid fearful sense, but in rejoicing over each new day given to us. The spiritual dimension to living is an area we may wish to develop in more depth.

Finding meaning in life is an issue I frequently find myself discussing with patients. Many times, when physical symptoms just won't go away, I engage the person in a conversation about life satisfaction. Often we unveil a sense of discontent with a job that is financially lucrative, but not providing any real meaning or joy. Or a longstanding relationship is not supportive and nurturing, but broken or false. Sometimes many issues are at play, and the person just is not thriving emotionally or spiritually, but it is their physical body that gives them the signals. As the philosopher Frederich Nietzsche said, _"Those who have a why to live can face most any how."_ We all need to feel our life is meaningful, to find the "why". When we can embrace our lives as truly meaningful and come to terms with the brevity of our existence, death moves from being a morbid concept that we shun, to one we become willing to face through valuing each day we have to live out our purpose.

4. What can medical organizations do?

Organized medicine (the American Medical Association, specialty societies, nursing organizations, and others) can decide its main commitment is to quality care for patients. While an organization's major reason to exist is often to protect and promote the interests of its members (doctors, nurses, retina specialists, and so on), this advocacy exists only in the context of protecting the public, our patients, or they have no actual purpose. As Roger Bulger recommended to academic health centers, the patient needs to be the focus of our existence.

Tainted Money for "Education"

Next, these organizations can decide that their educational programs and clinical information projects will not be contaminated by money from special interests. The pharmaceutical industry has an inordinate effect on what doctors learn about in their continuing medical education (CME) programs, largely because the companies supply "educational grants" to support these programs. While there are stringent controls on what can be dictated or not by the funding company, the choice of topics and speakers often gives a big slant to a company's particular interest. And it is intriguing to me that the vast preponderance of CME programs are centered on topics for which the only or major treatment options are pharmaceutical interventions. In truth, many, many conditions can be more effectively treated with nutritional or lifestyle interventions, but there is no one to fund such topics.

CME programs in American medicine today have aptly been described by many as "a joke." Having a large audience of doctors sit in a lecture hall for several hours listening to "experts" talk has never been shown to really change a physician's behavior in practice. Progressive organizations are looking into ways to individualize a doctor's continuing education to actually meet his or her needs for help in practicing more effectively. Having the pharmaceutical industry pay for this kind of individualized ongoing education program seems unlikely.

Recently, some food and beverage manufacturers have come forward to fund "obesity education" for professional medical organizations. These companies make products that are high in calories and high fructose corn syrup, but defend them as legitimate to promote, because people just need to exercise enough to maintain a healthy weight. They decline to admit that sugar and high fructose corn syrup are inflammatory messengers, and want us to consider them just like any other food with calories. Nothing could be further from the truth – 100 calories of sugar does not contain the same nutritional content as 100 calories of broccoli. Unfortunately, many prominent medical organizations are also buying this line of bunk, and making a lot of money in the process.

The big conventions that doctors of every specialty attend are a true three-ring circus for drug company advertising. Huge hotel and convention center exhibit halls are filled with display after extravagant display of companies competing for the doctor's attention (and ultimate prescription writing.) Sometimes famous celebrities or sports figures are recruited to sign autographs at the booths. Free food, cappuccino, brochures, canvas bags with gaudy logos, pens, notepads and other gimmicks from cheap to elegant are passed out as the doctors pass by. Sometimes even tickets to events or meals are distributed. Occasionally a lecturer holds forth inside a small classroom constructed within the display area to tout the company's product. The lines are long and deep for these freebies, especially when it's a cute teddy bear for the kids, or a set of golf balls. The medical organizations that sell these spaces to the drug companies will tell you that they could not hold the educational portion of their convention without this financial support from industry, and that the doctors would not be willing or able to pay for these meetings without such subsidies. I wonder how we will know this until at least one courageous medical organization tries it?

The nature of America's medical organizations would be dramatically different if tomorrow they started eschewing all monies from drug companies, equipment manufacturers, producers of unhealthy foods and beverages and others who have products they want doctors to prescribe, recommend or use. And in the big picture, American health care might be better off.

Political Leverage

Organized medicine could also begin working with school systems and hospitals to provide more nutritious food. And it could also work with the government to support subsidies for healthy, organic whole foods (fruits, vegetables, whole grains) and limit subsidies for tobacco, and for crops like corn that end up as poorly nutritious, but cheap refined carbohydrate products, so abundant in our food supply, and so unhealthy for us.

New Models of Care

Some innovations may be on the horizon if the plans of medical organizations like the American Academy of Family Physicians (AAFP) can actually be implemented. The AAFP has been working for several years on the Future of Family Medicine Project, hoping to create some new models of care that will help family doctors stay viable into the future. This project has many aspects, some of which might be considered "tinkering around the edges" such as group visits for chronic conditions, electronic medical records, and same day appointments. On the other hand, it promotes "patient-centered care," a "personal medical home," and a "whole-person orientation." These latter characteristics certainly resonate with what has been said in this book about changing our system to have a more holistic focus and bring the patient into the health care team.

The biggest problem with plans such as these, laudable as they are, is that they are about making the doctors (in this case the specialty of family medicine) relevant and viable, not about fundamentally changing the way health care is conceived and delivered. In the big picture of health care reform and improved access we may have different kinds of doctors with different names. This should not frighten us. As long as people require a professional who is trained to do the things they want help with, there will always be a need for us, no matter what we are called.

My friend and colleague, Joe Scherger, MD is a family physician with vision. He gave a lecture at the annual meeting of the Society of Teachers of Family Medicine in 2005 in which he spoke plainly about "the urgent need for radical change in family medicine if it is to survive in the US health system." His premise is that working harder in the same ineffective model we currently have, where a doctor's care is divided into 15 minute "visits," borders on "insanity;" i.e. doing things the same way over and over and expecting a different result. He proposes eliminating the concept of the "office visit" and turn to "productive interactions between informed, activated patients and a prepared, proactive practice team." These interactions could be on the Internet, telephone, in the office, in the patient's home, in group visits or educational sessions – wherever the most "productive" interaction can occur. And the doctor would be paid for his or her time, regardless of the setting.

Some examples of this type of practice are beginning to occur around the country. One is Alan Dappen, a family doctor in Virginia, who started a practice where he has about 1,000 active patients, sees 4 to 5 patients a day in the office in unhurried visits, handles about 20 patient messages daily, does a few house calls in a week. He charges for his time regardless of setting. Another example is Charles Kilo, an internist in Oregon who spends a half day each day seeing patients for 30 minutes each in the office, then the other half day messaging with patients over e-mail or telephone. The office is also used for patient education classes. Patients pay an annual fee to be a member of this practice. Even Kaiser, a huge health care organization, is developing Health Connect, an on-line platform in which patients can communicate with their providers, receive customized health information, arrange for services and review their health record.

If medical organizations would begin to really promote these new models of care, primary care practice could be transformed. The key to effective changes is that they are done because they serve the patient better. In my view these new models will be even more effective if we incorporate additional members on our team of health professionals and if the physical environments we utilize when we actually see people are more healing.

5.   What can payers do?

First, payers can relinquish control of medical decisions to the people who are trained to make them - doctors and other health professionals. The managers and clerks or reviewers can certainly help educate physicians about the costs of various options, and provide information on effectiveness of various choices, but the current adversarial interaction that so often occurs between physicians and case reviewers for insurance companies could transform into a real educational encounter on both sides.

The insurance companies, HMOs, PPOs and other types of health plans can offer "products" that provide options and choices to people. They might consider providing incentives or discounts to people who live healthy lifestyles, even if they have serious health problems. A person who has had a heart attack and who quits smoking should perhaps have a premium reduction, just as some companies provide lower rates to non-smokers and safe drivers who are healthy.

Unfortunately, a current theme in insurance payment seems to be that the **doctor** should be rewarded or punished for the health outcomes his or her patients experience. This is called "pay-for-performance" and is being seriously considered by Medicare. In other words, a doctor could practice very good medicine, using all the best guidelines available for managing a chronic condition such as diabetes, and yet the patient could decide not to eat the proper diet, not take his or her medication properly and have his or her diabetes get out of control. In a "pay-for-performance" scenario, the doctor would have his or her payment reduced for that patient's care, because the person's health outcome was not an improvement in the diabetes, but a worsening.

Another perhaps less Machiavellian version of pay-for-performance is following whether the doctor ordered the proper tests on patients, such as screening mammograms, pap smears for women of certain ages and hemoglobin A1c tests for diabetics. This approach is another backwards sort of band-aid measure to try to fix our broken system by cutting costs in the wrong way. It is true that we have a wide variation in health care practice today, and a wide variety in outcomes for any given disease or condition. Part of the solution is to help doctors know the "best practices," and give us evidence-based guidelines to help us practice excellent medicine. But our system keeps omitting the critical role the *patient* plays in caring for him or herself, and the responsibility each person has for taking care of him or herself. It may be because this approach seems more difficult than targeting the doctor or it's something we just haven't done before. And by the way, early research on this pay-for-performance idea is showing little improvement in quality. Again, we may be just "tinkering around the edges" with these proposals.

Payers need to find ways to support and reward patients for making good health care decisions. An article in the AMA's weekly news magazine described the Swiss health insurance system in which a person purchases insurance for five years at a time. If the person's health status is better at the end of five years, that person gets a percentage of the premium refunded. Now there's an incentive program to get people to practice better health habits! Why couldn't we do something similar here in the U.S.?

In fact, in a sort of reverse variation on this theme of rewarding people for adopting healthy lifestyles, King County in Washington State recently agreed with labor unions that county employees will pay $1,000 more annually in out-of-pocket expenses if they do not adopt healthy lifestyles and manage their chronic diseases well. We may begin to see more rewards and/or punitive measures being directed at patients themselves; again underlining a need for more personal responsibility in health care.

Misdirected Reimbursement?

We financially reward the end stage treatments, and discourage the up front patient education, counseling and preventive activities that might really lower our overall health care costs. Paying more for prevention would be a dramatic shift for payers, who still reward technical procedures with high dollars, while the physicians and nurses who offer preventive services and lifestyle counseling are paid far less for those types of services. And often, many insurance companies will deny a patient's claim if one of the diagnostic codes the doctor used for the visit is something considered "preventive."

In the AAFP's proposed new model of care health promotion, disease prevention, patient education and support for self-care are all core services the family physician would offer. We do these things now, but we don't get paid for it.

"Mismanaged" Care

The concept of managed care had much to commend it at the outset. The stated purpose was to help organize care better so patients could get the proper service at the proper time, instead of running hither and yon to doctors and specialists they might not really need. The originators of this type of care felt that costs would be saved because prevention, education and primary care would become keystones, and chronic diseases could be managed in a population context. Unfortunately, costs continued to escalate and managers began to have to manage costs rather than care. Now we are experiencing all the problems of a system based on a bottom line mentality.

Payers, too, need to be open to the health benefits and even financial savings that could be achieved with proper integration of complementary therapies. Few insurance plans currently cover much in the way of non-allopathic medical approaches. A few are beginning to see benefits in health outcomes and costs when judicious use of body work, acupuncture, chiropractic, yoga, mind-body medicine and others are incorporated into the therapeutic tool box.

Payers would transform our system if they decided to pay for services based on their value to the overall system, rather than more money for more surgical and other interventionist procedures. We are all well aware that a surgeon receives tens of thousands of dollars for performing an open-heart surgery, but the doctors and health educators who work with patients to lower their risk of heart disease are paid a pittance.

6. What can health care company executives do?

Health care executives are a subset of health professionals. They, too, need to reassess their personal values, and become "principle-centered leaders." This is a term Steven Covey, a noted author and speaker, has made popular in the business world. Organizations succeed if the leadership has clear values and principles and live them in every decision they make every day. Leaders set the tone and ethic of the organization. Health care executives can transform health care itself if they align their organizational goals with their personal ethics.

They could decide not to work in for-profit systems, as these tend to put the interests of shareholders and return-on-investment above the need to provide quality services to humans in need. One such executive was Dr. Linda Peeno, whose poignant experience ran as the cover story in *US News and World Report* on March 9, 1998. Dr. Peeno was an HMO executive from 1987 to 1991. She finally left after a particularly difficult case in which she was pressured by numerous non-physician staffers to deny an expensive voice machine for a young patient who had suffered a stroke that left her unable to speak. She was shocked that some of those urging her to deny the machine indicated that she would be spending everyone's money, including employees of the health plan who stood to receive bonuses from the health plan's financial success. Physicians and non-physician executives of these companies need to follow Dr. Peeno's example and get out of companies that put profit over care.

7.   What can employers do?

Employers can look at the situation today from an historical perspective. Before World War II, health insurance was not a benefit related to employment. But, during the war, there was a labor shortage, and the government also imposed a wage freeze. The only way employers could attract and keep good employees was by providing non-wage benefits, such as health insurance. Over the years, employee groups lobbied for more benefits so better and more comprehensive health plans became the norm. We are one of the few developed countries in the world where health coverage is linked to employment, rather than being a tax-covered universal benefit. Employers could work with employee groups and government representatives to help design a better system. Most employers would probably be happy to get out of the health benefits management business. These activities consume increasing amounts of time, energy and money on the part of employers, detracting from their ability to put that time, energy and money into managing their actual business.

Employers could decide to provide equivalent salary increases to the amounts currently being paid for health benefits, and allow employees to purchase their own plans. Or they could offer a high deductible catastrophic plan and contribute cash to the employee's health savings account. Our current situation that allows large employers to have a purchasing advantage over a single individual would have to be overcome with purchasing cooperatives or some other way to offer affordable premiums to workers. A simplistic approach would be for the US to have a single payer system, like many Western European countries and Canada, but this scenario seems unlikely in our current cultural and political environment.

In simpler ways, employers can encourage healthy behaviors that will make their workforce less susceptible to illness and help them be less likely to develop a costly chronic health condition. Many larger employers have gyms and exercise facilities on the premises, and even offer classes in aerobics, yoga and stress management. Some offer healthy foods in their cafeterias and vending machines offered at lower prices than unhealthy choices, and many companies have become non-smoking environments. Some have health clinics on site. All of these efforts are laudable, and some companies are finding bottom line savings with these activities.

Pitney Bowes in Stamford, Connecticut offers a "Health Care University" where employees attend classes and earn points toward lowering the amount they pay for health insurance, and are offered lower prices on drugs needed to treat chronic conditions like asthma or diabetes, to encourage using the drugs to prevent the condition from worsening. Participating workers' health costs are 10% lower than those who don't participate. And in another example of leadership being critical for organizational success in change, Pitney's CEO was quoted in USA Today on August 1, 2005: "We've got to create a culture in which healthy employees and families are valued. It does start with the CEO." According to the Health Management Research Center at the University of Michigan, employer-based wellness programs return $3 to the company's bottom line for every $1 invested in such programs.

8. What can government do?

Government officials and elected leaders can step up to the plate of making meaningful progress toward fixing our health care system. They may have to make overtures of cooperation to their political rivals so that true bipartisan solutions can be found. They need to create a workable plan to enfranchise all of our citizens into the health care system. So far, this concept has not been popular with politicians, but it is the right thing to do. Another quote from Gandhi about leadership seems apt here:

> *"A leader is useless when he acts against the prompting of his conscience, surrounded as he must be by people holding all kinds of views. He will drift like an anchorless ship if he has not the inner voice to hold him firm and to guide him."*

I truly believe that most of our elected leaders in their heart of hearts think that universal access to health care is something a resource-rich and generous nation like America should find a way to accomplish. I imagine they get sidetracked by special interests and "people holding all kinds of other views." If they could come back to their conscience about this essential aspect of our collective lives, I believe this problem can be solved.

Fiscal Considerations

If we are to have more autonomy and individually selected and owned health insurance, there will need to be changes in laws to permit tax credits for health insurance expenses. Currently, tax credits are only available to employers and employees for insurance plans selected and offered by the employer. If we are to encourage more autonomy and choice, these same tax benefits will need to be extended to individually owned and directed plans. Legislation has now been passed by our government representatives, but it is under fire for repeal by opponents. Our leaders will need to stand up to the big insurance industry, which does not want to change.

And What About Our Food Supply?

Those who govern can look at the role agricultural subsidies have played in creating an unequal playing field for growers to be able to sell affordable healthy foods. The cheapest foods in the grocery store are those that are high calorie, low nutrition products containing trans fatty acids and high fructose corn syrup. The most expensive foods are fruits and vegetables and high quality protein. Could government cut crop subsidies to corn growers and offer them to organic fruit and vegetable growers? Why not?? Not too many Americans think farm subsidies are anything that could be vaguely related to health care, yet they are wrong. Our biggest health care epidemic today is obesity and the serious health problems that accompany obesity: diabetes, hypertension, heart disease and stroke.

If we made healthy foods cheaper and poorly nutritious foods more expensive, perhaps we could be farther down the road towards healthy living in America.

Drugs, Drugs, Drugs....

Government must also be in a position to negotiate drug prices with the pharmaceutical industry. It is unconscionable that the exact same drugs manufactured by U.S. or international companies sold in the U.S. cost about 40% less when purchased in Canada. Carolyn, a delightful 70-year-old patient of mine, has discovered that a three month supply of her medications that cost $628 here cost her $290 when purchased in Canada. On average, patients in the US paid an average of 81% more for brand name prescription drugs than in Canada and six Western European countries in 2004, according to a report by Boston University School of Public Health.

Rather than our government spending their time and energy (i.e. **our** money that supports **their** time and energy) to block the availability of Canadian drugs, our leaders should be negotiating lower drug rates here in the U.S. and finding real ways to help people cover their medication costs. In 2010, about one quarter of non-elderly adult Americans lacked drug coverage. The state of Illinois alone spends over $3 billion annually on drugs for state employees, Medicaid beneficiaries, inmates in correctional facilities, mental health recipients and others covered by the public sector in that state. Their governor and legislature were motivated, as are many others, to find less expensive sources for these needed medications and have found ways to get them for their beneficiaries through Canada or the European Union and offer them via the internet for "personal importation" on their I-saveRx.net website.

The argument that is sometimes voiced about this scenario is that price controls on drugs would discourage the drug companies from being willing to invest research dollars into finding new cures for disease. There are several counter arguments to offer to this assertion:

1) The majority of new drugs on the market are not breakthrough new drugs for disease, they are copycat or "me-

too" drugs that make no significant impact on health improvement and are almost always more expensive.

2) Drug companies spend more money on marketing than research. Families USA reported in 2000 that the major international drug companies spent two to three times more of their revenue on marketing than on research. Bristol Myers-Squibb, for example, invested 30% of its revenue on marketing, while expending just 11% on research and development (R & D.) Merck allocated 15% of its revenue toward marketing, while expending just 6% on R & D.   Six percent of a company's revenue devoted to research and development is a paltry number in this business that complains its R & D costs are the reason for high prescription drug prices. Perhaps with lower profit margins, the pharmaceutical companies would have to decrease or eliminate the practice of direct-to-consumer advertising and drug detailing and samples to physicians.

3) Truly needed new drug research and drug production could continue to be supported by government grants and even, perhaps, by appropriate subsidies. Most drug company "research" actually originates with basic science work done by government funding through the National Institutes of Health, so the government (i.e. you and me) is already funding the greatest portion of the drug companies' "research" anyway.

Another relatively little known cost hike is the difference in pricing available from various pharmacies. A now infamous e-mail has circulated the country about the much lower pricing for generic drugs available from Costco than from most of the chain pharmacies. It really does pay to check around and compare prices, as the savings can be considerable. A budget analyst for the US Department of Commerce evidently originated this e-mail after finding the cost for a pain medication she was taking was $72.57 for 145 pills at CVS and only $28.08 for 150 pills at Costco. Again, price–setting is an arbitrary process, as we saw with hospital fees in Chapter 2.

9.   What can industry do?

The **_pharmaceutical companies_** could become the biggest heroes of all in the effort to fix our ailing system. If they seriously evaluated their role overall in health care, including their business of making money by selling drugs, they could create a major transformation. What if they all decided not to pursue direct-to-consumer advertising? What if they decided not to pay their sales reps six-figure incomes (as much or more than many physicians' incomes)? What if they did not give away free samples to doctors and then actually lowered their prices substantially based on all these cost savings? "Very naive" you are saying now. Probably so. But think of the money they would save on buying off politicians to promote their economic interests in Washington. It would even make the politicians look better to us!

To put this issue of buying off our politicians into perspective, in 2002 there were 675 pharmaceutical lobbyists in Washington, DC. That year, drug companies spent $91 million on lobbying our government officials to pass legislation preferential to their interests (or blocking legislation that might hurt them economically.) Between 1997 and 2005, a total of $675 million was spent by the pharmaceutical industry on lobbying in Washington. Its lobbying money and campaign contributions are exceeded only by those from the insurance industry.

And how can the pharmaceutical industry really justify the horrendous costs of certain drugs? *Business Week* on January 30, 2006 ran an article about the cost of cancer treatment titled "Going Broke to Stay Alive." It highlighted Avastin, a drug used for certain types of colon, lung, breast and ovarian cancer that costs $4,400 to $8,800 per month. Herceptin, another drug used for breast cancer runs $3,200 a month, and anti-nausea drugs to relieve a common side effect of cancer treatment can cost $100 *per pill*. Patients have been known to mortgage their homes to cover the costs of these expensive treatments.

But these hugely expensive drugs are unique and have patent protection for many years, so the manufacturer has no incentive to reduce the price. In addition, Medicare has been forbidden from negotiating prices with drug companies as a condition of the new Medicare Part D prescription drug plan. A pretty fantastic deal for the drug companies, no? Can those CEOs sleep at night? They probably have to take an expensive sleeping pill.

But drug companies are big employers. Aren't they having difficulties with health benefit costs skyrocketing? Aren't they concerned about the costs of drugs within the health plans they pay for? And everyone that works in a drug company, from the CEO on down, is a human being in our society, and has certain ethical obligations to everyone else.

The **_media_** has a role to play as well. TV, radio and print and on-line media executives could make some decisions that could help. What if they stopped taking pharmaceutical ads? Sure, their revenue might drop, but perhaps so would their employees' drug costs. And, if it isn't really ethical to advertise prescription drugs to consumers, perhaps they could step up to the ethics plate, too, just like doctors, health care executives, government officials. We're all in this mess together.

What about **_agribusiness?_** How about them lobbying for subsidies for healthy foods instead of corn? (Coming from Kansas, I am on shaky ground asking to decrease corn subsidies.) Corn is a wonderful food. But most corn that is grown is not eaten off the cob with barbeque and homemade strawberry shortcake. Most of it goes to make high fructose corn syrup that is added to all sorts of processed foods and becomes a high calorie, non-nutrient staple in the American diet, as it is cheap to consumers (because it is subsidized...) and it tastes good. Could agribusiness get on a health kick and support the farming of healthy crops in order to make them cheaper?

Speaking of corn subsidies, perhaps they could still be supported if a large percentage of the corn grown in America were used to produce ethanol as an alternative fuel source for automobiles and not for high fructose corn syrup.

And agribusiness could be looking more seriously at the money to be made from herbal crops, as herbal medicine is becoming more and more sought after by the American public. On a positive note for Kansas agriculture, the best Echinacea in the world grows in Kansas. Efforts are underway to develop the capacity to grow useful natural and herbal remedies in my own state, a wonderful direction for agribusiness.

And what about the ***food and beverage industry***? They need to stop lying to the public, medical professional societies and themselves that their products are to be considered only in the context of "calories in, calories out" and start making healthier foods that actually have nutritional value and not continue to be among the major contributors to the obesity epidemic.

So, we **all** are travelers on the road to change. As Edward Deming, a noted business management thought leader has observed in *The Fourteen Obligations of Management:*

1. Just because we've always done something doesn't mean it actually works now or ever did.
2. We cannot solve problems by doing the same thing harder. We will have to do something different.
3. It doesn't matter how well people do the wrong thing.
4. As a manager/supervisor, I do not "change" other people's behavior. I can only change my behavior. Others will respond to the changes I make in my behavior.

So, like managers in an organization, or like people in dysfunctional relationships or like Mahatma Gandhi, if we want things to be different, we have to change ourselves first. Doctors may have to make some different decisions about their practices; patients may have to change their lifestyles and possibly their expectations about having everything. Politicians may have to listen to their consciences and support a health care system that includes us all; drug companies may have to make less money. Hospitals may have to transform into true healing environments and medical schools may have to change their focus and the content of their curricula. Not all of these things will happen overnight, and many may never happen. Everyone in every role has an opportunity to make a difference. It will be difficult, and frightening to create a new health care system, and, as Machiavelli observed in *The Prince*:

> *"There is nothing more difficult to take in hand, more perilous to conduct, or more uncertain in its success, than to take the lead in the introduction of a new order of things."*

Health care in America is ripe for change. Even though perilous, let's begin.

The time is now to be the change you wish to see in the world.

EPILOGUE

2010 finally brought us a beginning of much needed health care reform in America. What we got, actually, are incremental insurance reforms and enhanced access for uninsured Americans – both important steps toward improved health care. But these reforms have also brought forth serious political divisions and arguments against change, primarily based on fear and perceived loss of individual control. Change is always difficult and frightening. The devil we know somehow seems safer than the devil we don't.

Yet even insured Americans have been very unhappy with health care for decades. Many of us have felt like victims of the insurance companies' denials of benefits, rejecting our applications due to pre-existing conditions, and those ever-escalating health insurance premiums. We patients have grudgingly gone along with selecting a new physician each year as our employer changes our insurance plan. We ask for pills for our ills instead of taking responsibility for our lifestyle choices. We physicians continue to work for big health systems, hospitals and medical groups and collect our paychecks while silently wondering, "Is that all there is?" in terms of personal and professional fulfillment. Deep discontent pervades the system we have known for years.

And while we finally have some legislation to begin the process of changing the structure of health care in America, we must begin to realize that each participant in the system – patients, health professionals, employers, insurance company executives, legislators - needs to change our own expectations and change our own behavior. No system can transform unless we each modify our behavior.

I am learning it is possible to rediscover the heart and soul of medicine. I am learning that many techniques and philosophies that were not taught in medical school can sometimes be more helpful to some patients than the tools my Western medicine can offer.

I have dreams for a reborn and re-humanized health care system: One that honors the values of individuality and healing relationships along with the life-saving technologies we have at our disposal. We should be able to do all this in the context of population health as well. I see a new kind of hospital in the future, a new kind of medical school, and a new kind of payment system that expects a high degree of personal responsibility, and offers a high degree of autonomy in return.

What can we do to reach these dreams? We each will have to change. We will have to make personal decisions as health professionals how we choose to practice. Health care executives will have to choose what kind of organizations they want to manage and in which they really want to work. Government officials will have to decide that making the right decisions for the greatest good may be difficult, but necessary and worthwhile. Consumers will have to decide how much responsibility for their own health and health care costs they will accept, and that there are always limits to what we may want.

If we want true change, we each must **be** the change.

GLOSSARY

Acupuncture : An ancient practice that uses very thin needles inserted at specific points in the body, along "meridians" or energy channels, to access the body's "chi" (qi) or vital energy. Much research has been undertaken in recent years, including studies funded by the National Institutes of Health (NIH) to better understand the effects and potential effectiveness of this technique. More information can be obtained from the National Commission for the Certification of Acupuncture and Chinese Medicine (NCCAOM) at www.nccaom.org regarding training and certification requirements. Physicians, chiropractors and naturopaths often include acupuncture in their practices. They usually have training that differs from that required of a NCCAOM certified individual.

Agency for Healthcare Research & Quality (AHRQ): An agency in the federal government that reviews research on quality parameters in health care and develops quality of care guidelines for the medical community. www.ahrq.gov

Allopathic medicine: Type of medicine studied to attain the MD (Medical Doctor) degree. "Allo" means "other" or "different from"; "pathy" meaning disease - and contrasts with other approaches to healing such as "osteo" meaning "bone or skeletal structure", "homeo" meaning "alike", "naturo" meaning using natural approaches to healing.

American Academy of Family Physicians (AAFP): the largest national medical specialty society in the U.S. Represents over 90,000 family physicians, residents in training and medical students. www.aafp.org

Art Therapy: a mental health profession that uses the creative process of art making to improve and enhance the physical, mental and emotional well-being of individuals of all ages. It is based on the belief that the creative process involved in artistic self-expression helps people to resolve conflicts and problems, develop interpersonal skills, manage behavior, reduce stress, increase self-esteem and self-awareness, and achieve insight. www.arttherapy.org

Association of Academic Health Centers (AAHC): a non-profit organization that seeks to advance the nation's health and well-being through vigorous leadership of the nation's academic health centers. Such centers include university-based hospitals and medical schools. www.aahcdc.org

Association of American Medical Colleges(AAMC): the AAMC represents all 133 accredited U.S. and 17 accredited Canadian medical schools; approximately 400 major teaching hospitals and health systems, including 68 Department of Veterans Affairs medical centers; and nearly 90 academic and scientific societies. Through these institutions and organizations, the AAMC represents 125,000 faculty members, 75,000 medical students, and 106,000 resident physicians. www.aamc.org

Ayurvedic Medicine: Ayurvedic medicine (also called Ayurveda) is one of the world's oldest medical systems. It originated in India and has evolved there over thousands of years. The term "Ayurveda" combines the Sanskrit words *ayur* (life) and *veda* (science or knowledge). Thus, Ayurveda means "the science of life." In the United States, Ayurvedic medicine is considered a type of CAM and a whole medical system. As with other such systems, it is based on theories of health and illness and on ways to prevent, manage, or treat health problems. Ayurvedic medicine aims to integrate and balance the body, mind, and spirit; thus, some view it as "holistic." This balance is believed to lead to happiness and health, and to help prevent illness. Ayurvedic medicine also treats specific physical and mental health problems. A chief aim of Ayurvedic practices is to cleanse the body of substances that can cause disease, thus helping to reestablish harmony and balance.
www.nccam.nih.gov/health/ayurveda

Beneficiary: The person who receives the benefits of an insurance policy.

Biofeedback: Biofeedback is a complementary and alternative medicine technique in which you learn to control bodily functions, such as your heart rate, using your mind. With biofeedback, you're connected to electrical sensors that help you measure and receive information (feedback) about your body (bio). The biofeedback sensors teach you how to make subtle changes in your body, such as relaxing certain muscles, to achieve the results you want, such as reducing pain. In essence, biofeedback gives you the power to use your thoughts to control your body, often to help with a health condition or physical performance. Biofeedback is often used as a relaxation technique. http://www.mayoclinic.com/health/biofeedback/MY01072

Chakra: Chakras are energy centers of the physical and metaphysical body. They are the openings for life energy to flow into and out of our aura. Their function is to vitalize the physical body and to bring about the development of our self-consciousness. They are associated with our physical, mental and emotional interactions.

Chiropractor: Chiropractic is a health care profession that focuses on disorders of the musculoskeletal system and the nervous system, and the effects of these disorders on general health. Chiropractic care is used most often to treat neuromusculoskeletal complaints, including but not limited to back pain, neck pain, pain in the joints of the arms or legs, and headaches. Doctors of Chiropractic – often referred to as chiropractors or chiropractic physicians – practice a drug-free, hands-on approach to health care that includes patient examination, diagnosis and treatment. Chiropractors have broad diagnostic skills and are also trained to recommend therapeutic and rehabilitative exercises, as well as to provide nutritional, dietary and lifestyle counseling. www.acatoday.org

COBRA: The Consolidated Omnibus Budget Reconciliation Act (COBRA) gives workers and their families who lose their health benefits the right to choose to continue group health benefits provided by their group health plan for limited periods of time under certain circumstances such as voluntary or involuntary job loss, reduction in the hours worked, transition between jobs, death, divorce, and other life events. Qualified individuals may be required to pay the entire premium for coverage up to 102 percent of the cost to the plan. www.dol.gov/ebsa/cobra

Commonweal: Commonweal is a nonprofit health and environmental research institute in Bolinas, California. Founded in 1976, Commonweal conducts programs that contribute to human and ecosystem health — to a safer world for people and for all life. www.commonweal.org

Complementary/Alternative Medicine (CAM): Defining CAM is difficult, because the field is very broad and constantly changing. NCCAM defines CAM as a group of diverse medical and health care systems, practices, and products that are not generally considered part of conventional medicine. Conventional medicine (also called Western or allopathic medicine) is medicine as practiced by holders of M.D. (medical doctor) and D.O. (doctor of osteopathy) degrees and by allied health professionals, such as physical therapists, psychologists, and registered nurses. The boundaries between CAM and conventional medicine are not absolute, and specific CAM practices may, over time, become widely accepted. "Complementary medicine" refers to use of CAM **together with** conventional medicine, such as using acupuncture in addition to usual care to help lessen pain. Most use of CAM by Americans is complementary. "Alternative medicine" refers to use of CAM **in place of** conventional medicine. www.nccam.nih.gov

Consortium of Academic Health Centers for Integrative Medicine: The mission of the Consortium is to advance the principles and practices of integrative healthcare within academic institutions. The Consortium provides its institutional membership with a community of support for their academic missions and a collective voice for influencing change. www.ahc.umn.edu/cahcim

Consumer-Driven Health Care: refers to health insurance plans that allow members to use personal Health Saving Accounts (HSAs), Health Reimbursement Arrangements (HRAs), or similar medical payment products to pay routine health care expenses directly, while a high-deductible health insurance policy protects them from catastrophic medical expenses. High-deductible policies cost less, but the user pays routine medical claims using a pre-funded spending account, often with a special debit card provided by a bank or insurance plan. If the balance on this account runs out, the user then pays claims just like under a regular deductible. Users keep any unused balance or "rollover" at the end of the year to increase future balances, or to invest for future expenses. This system of health care is referred to as "consumer driven health care" because routine claims are paid using a consumer-controlled account versus a fixed health insurance benefit. That gives patients greater control over their own health budgets.

Craniosacral Therapy: is a gentle, hands-on method of evaluating and enhancing the functioning of a physiological body system called the craniosacral system - comprised of the membranes and cerebrospinal fluid that surround and protect the brain and spinal cord. Using a soft touch generally no greater than 5 grams, or about the weight of a nickel, practitioners release restrictions in the craniosacral system to improve the functioning of the central nervous system.
www.craniosacraltherapy.org

Dosha: According to ayurveda, the five fundamental elements that make up the universe - space (akasha), air (vayu), fire (agni), water (apu) and earth (prithvi) - also make up the human physiology. Ayurveda describes three biological humors or psychophysiological energies called doshas. There are three doshas, called Vata, Pitta and Kapha, and each is mainly a combination of two elements. Vata dosha is made up of space and air. Pitta dosha is a combination of fire and water. Kapha dosha is made up of water and earth. Each of these doshas is further divided into five sub-doshas. Together, the doshas orchestrate all the activities that occur within us.

Emotional Intelligence (EI): the ability, capacity or skill to identify, assess, and control the emotions of one's self, of others, and of groups. EI is often used in leadership and business settings to identify those who may be more prepared to lead and mange skillfully.

Energy Medicine: includes all energetic and informational interactions resulting from self-regulation or brought about through other energy couplings to mind and body. In addition to various therapeutic energies that may be used, there are also energy pulses from the environment that influence humans and animals in a variety of ways. For instance, low level changes in magnetic, electric, electromagnetic, acoustic, and gravitational fields often have profound effects on both biology and psychology. In addition to energies originating in the environment, it has been documented that humans are capable of generating and controlling subtle not-yet-measurable energies that seem to influence both physiologic and physical mechanisms. www.issseem.org

Family Medicine: Family medicine is the medical specialty that provides continuing, comprehensive health care for the individual and family. It is a specialty in breadth that integrates the biological, clinical and behavioral sciences. The scope of family medicine encompasses all ages, both sexes, each organ system and every disease entity. A physician must complete a 3-year residency program following medical school to be eligible to become board certified in family medicine. Family physicians must maintain certification with ongoing continuing education, practice evaluation and cognitive testing every 7-10 years. www.aafp.org

Families USA: Families USA is a national nonprofit, non-partisan organization dedicated to the achievement of high-quality, affordable health care for all Americans. Working at the national, state, and community levels, we have earned a national reputation as an effective voice for health care consumers for 25 years. www.familiesusa.org

Fibromyalgia: Fibromyalgia is a chronic condition characterized by widespread pain in your muscles, ligaments and tendons, as well as fatigue and multiple tender points — places on your body where slight pressure causes pain. Fibromyalgia occurs in about 2 percent of the population in the United States. Women are much more likely to develop the disorder than are men, and the risk of fibromyalgia increases with age. Fibromyalgia symptoms often begin after a physical or emotional trauma, but in many cases there appears to be no triggering event. www.mayoclinic.com/health/fibromyalgia/DS00079

Functional Medicine: is personalized medicine that deals with primary prevention and underlying causes instead of symptoms for serious chronic disease. It is a science-based field of health care that is grounded in the following principles: **Biochemical individuality** describes the importance of individual variations in metabolic function that derive from genetic and environmental differences among individuals. **Patient-centered** medicine emphasizes "patient care" rather than "disease care," following Sir William Osler's admonition that "It is more important to know what patient has the disease than to know what disease the patient has. **Dynamic balance** of internal and external factors. **Web-like interconnections** of physiological factors – an abundance of research now supports the view that the human body functions as an orchestrated network of interconnected systems, rather than individual systems functioning autonomously and without affect on each other. For example, we now know that immunological dysfunctions can promote cardiovascular disease, that dietary imbalances can cause hormonal disturbances, and that environmental exposures can precipitate neurologic syndromes such as Parkinson's disease. **Health as a positive vitality** – not merely the absence of disease. **Promotion of organ reserve** as the means to enhance health span. www.functionalmedicine.org

Gandhi, Mohandas K. (Mahatma): was born on October 2, 1869 in Porbandar, India; he was assassinated on January 30, 1948 in Delhi. He became one of the most respected spiritual and political leaders of the twentieth century. Gandhi helped free the Indian people from British rule through nonviolent resistance, and is honored by his people as the father of the Indian Nation. The Indian people called Gandhi Mahatma, meaning Great Soul.

Guided Imagery: is a program of directed thoughts and suggestions that guide your imagination toward a relaxed, focused state. You can use an instructor, tapes, or scripts to help you through this process. Guided imagery is based on the concept that your body and mind are connected. Using all of your senses, your body seems to respond as though what you are imagining is real. An example often used is to imagine an orange or a lemon in great detail-the smell, the color, the texture of the peel. Continue to imagine the smell of the lemon, and then see yourself taking a bite of the lemon and feel the juice squirting into your mouth. Many people salivate when they do this. This exercise demonstrates how your body can respond to what you are imagining.

Health Maintenance Organization (HMO): A form of health insurance combining a range of coverage on a group basis. A group of doctors and other medical professionals offer care through the HMO for a flat monthly rate with no deductibles. However, only visits to professionals within the HMO network are covered by the policy. All visits, prescriptions and other care must be cleared by the HMO in order to be covered. A primary physician within the HMO handles referrals.

Health Savings Account (HSA): A Health Savings Account is an alternative to traditional health insurance; it is a savings product that offers a different way for consumers to pay for their health care. HSAs enable you to pay for current health expenses and save for future qualified medical and retiree health expenses on a tax-free basis. You must be covered by a High Deductible Health Plan (HDHP) to be able to take advantage of HSAs. An HDHP generally costs less than what traditional health care coverage costs, so the money that you save on insurance can therefore be put into the Health Savings Account.   You own and you control the money in your HSA. Decisions on how to spend the money are made by you without relying on a third party or a health insurer. You will also decide what types of investments to make with the money in the account in order to make it grow. www.ustreas.gov/offices/public-affairs/hsa

Holistic Medicine: Holistic medicine is the art and science of healing that addresses care of the whole person - body, mind, and spirit. The practice of holistic medicine integrates conventional and complementary therapies to promote optimal health, and prevent and treat disease by addressing contributing factors. In practice, this means that each person is seen as a unique individual, rather than an example of a particular disease. Disease is understood to be the result of physical, emotional, spiritual, social and environmental imbalance. Healing, therefore, takes place naturally when these aspects of life are brought into proper balance. The role of the practitioner is as guide, mentor and role model; the patient must do the work - changing lifestyle, beliefs and old habits in order to facilitate healing. All appropriate methods may be used, from medication to meditation. www.holisticmedicine.org

Homeopathy: Homeopathy, also known as homeopathic medicine is a whole medical system that was developed in Germany more than 200 years ago and has been practiced in the United States since the early 19th century. Homeopathy is used for wellness and prevention and to treat many diseases and conditions. The principle of similars (or "like cures like") is a central homeopathic principle. The principle states that a disease can be cured by a homeopathically prepared substance that, in it's unaltered form, produces similar symptoms in healthy people. http://nccam.nih.gov/health/homeopathy/

Hypnosis: Hypnosis, also referred to as hypnotherapy or hypnotic suggestion, is a trance-like state in which you have heightened focus, concentration and inner absorption. When you're under hypnosis, you usually feel calm and relaxed, and you can concentrate intensely on a specific thought, memory, feeling or sensation while blocking out distractions. Under hypnosis, you're more open than usual to suggestions, and this can be used to modify your perceptions, behavior, sensations and emotions. Therapeutic hypnosis is used to improve your health and well being and is different from so-called stage hypnosis used by entertainers. Although you're more open to suggestion during therapeutic hypnosis, your free will remains intact and you don't lose control over your behavior.
www.mayoclinic.com/health/hypnosis/MY01020

Institute for Healthcare Improvement (IHI): The Institute for Healthcare Improvement (IHI) is an independent not-for-profit organization helping to lead the improvement of health care throughout the world. Founded in 1991 and based in Cambridge, Massachusetts, IHI works to accelerate improvement by building the will for change, cultivating promising concepts for improving patient care, and helping health care systems put those ideas into action. www.ihi.org

Institute of Medicine (IOM): The Institute of Medicine (IOM) is an independent, nonprofit organization that works outside of government to provide unbiased and authoritative advice to decision makers and the public. Established in 1970, the IOM is the health arm of the National Academy of Sciences, which was chartered under President Abraham Lincoln in 1863. Nearly 150 years later, the National Academy of Sciences has expanded into what is collectively known as the National Academies, which comprises the National Academy of Sciences, the National Academy of Engineering, the National Research Council, and the IOM. www.iom.edu

Integrative Medicine: Integrative medicine (also called integrated medicine) refers to a practice that combines both conventional and CAM treatments for which there is evidence of safety and effectiveness. www.nccam.nih.gov

Kaiser Family Foundation: a non-profit, private operating foundation focusing on the major health care issues facing the

U.S., as well as the U.S. role in global health policy. Unlike grant-making foundations, Kaiser develops and runs its own research and communications programs, sometimes in partnership with other non-profit research organizations or major media companies. We serve as a non-partisan source of facts, information, and analysis for policymakers, the media, the health care community, and the public. Our product is information, always provided free of charge — from the most sophisticated policy research, to basic facts and numbers, to information young people can use to improve their health or elderly people can use to understand their Medicare benefits. The Kaiser Family Foundation is not associated with Kaiser Permanente or Kaiser Industries. www.kff.org

Managed Care: Managed care plans are health insurance plans that contract with health care providers and medical facilities to provide care for members at reduced costs. These providers make up the plan's network. How much of your care the plan will pay for depends on the network's rules. Restrictive plans generally cost you less. More flexible plans cost more. There are three types of managed care plans: *Health Maintenance Organizations (HMO)* usually only pay for care within the network. You choose a primary care doctor who coordinates most of your care. *Preferred Provider Organizations (PPO)* usually pay more if you get care within the network, but they still pay a portion if you go outside. *Point of Service (POS) plans* let you choose between an HMO or a PPO each time you need care. www.nlm.nih.gov

Massage Therapy: The term "massage therapy" encompasses many different techniques. In general, therapists press, rub, and otherwise manipulate the muscles and other soft tissues of the body. They most often use their hands and fingers, but may use their forearms, elbows, or feet. www.nccam.nih.gov

Medicare: Medicare is our country's health insurance program for people age 65 or older. Certain people younger than age 65 can qualify for Medicare, too, including those who have disabilities and those who have permanent kidney failure or amyotrophic lateral sclerosis (Lou Gehrig's disease). The program helps with the cost of health care, but it does not cover all medical expenses or the cost of most long-term care. Medicare is financed by a portion of the payroll taxes paid by workers and their employers. It also is financed in part by monthly premiums deducted from Social Security checks. www.medicare.gov

Medicaid: Medicaid is the U.S. health program for eligible individuals and families with low incomes and resources. It is a means tested program that is jointly funded by the state and federal governments, and is managed by the states. Among the groups of people served by Medicaid are certain eligible U.S. citizens and resident aliens, including low-income adults and their children, and people with certain disabilities. Poverty alone does not necessarily qualify an individual for Medicaid. Medicaid is the largest source of funding for medical and health-related services for people with limited income in the United States. Because of the aging World War II/Korean generation, the fastest growing aspect of Medicaid is nursing home coverage. As the Baby Boomer generation begins to reach nursing home age in 2020 to 2040, the nursing home aspect of Medicaid will boom, causing concerns for federal and state budgets. www.cms.gov

Mind-Body Practices: Mind-body practices focus on the interactions among the brain, mind, body, and behavior, with the intent to use the mind to affect physical functioning and promote health. Many CAM practices embody this concept—in different ways. www.nccam.nih.gov

Mindfulness Meditation: Mindfulness is a type of meditation that essentially involves focusing on your mind on the present. To be mindful is to be aware of your thoughts and actions in the present, without judging yourself.

Medical Savings Account (MSA): A medical plan combining high-deductible medical insurance protection with a tax-deferred savings account that can be offered by employers as part of a benefits package. Medical savings accounts are designed to help participants pay for medical and healthcare expenses by allowing them to save for those expenses in a tax-sheltered environment. Participants pay healthcare expenses from this account up to the amount of the insurance deductible. (see **Health Savings Account**)

Music Therapy: Music Therapy is the clinical and evidence-based use of music interventions to accomplish individualized goals within a therapeutic relationship by a credentialed professional who has completed an approved music therapy program. www.musictherapy.org

National Center for Complementary & Alternative Medicine (NCCAM): the National Center for Complementary and Alternative Medicine (NCCAM) is the Federal Government's lead agency for scientific research on the diverse medical and health care systems, practices, and products that are not generally considered part of conventional medicine. www.nccam.nih.gov

National Center for Health Statistics (NCHS): As the Nation's principal health statistics agency, we compile statistical information to guide actions and policies to improve the health of our people. We are a unique public resource for health information - a critical element of public health and health policy. www.cdc.gov/nchs

National Institutes of Health (NIH): NIH's mission is to seek fundamental knowledge about the nature and behavior of living systems and the application of that knowledge to enhance health, lengthen life, and reduce the burdens of illness and disability. The NIH invests over $31.2* billion annually in medical research for the American people. More than 80% of the NIH's funding is awarded through almost 50,000 competitive grants to more than 325,000 researchers at over 3,000 universities, medical schools, and other research institutions in every state and around the world. About 10% of the NIH's budget supports projects conducted by nearly 6,000 scientists in its own laboratories, most of which are on the NIH campus in Bethesda, Maryland. www.nih.gov

Naturopathic Medicine: Naturopathic medicine is based on the belief that the human body has an innate healing ability. Naturopathic doctors (NDs) teach their patients to use diet, exercise, lifestyle changes and cutting edge natural therapies to enhance their bodies' ability to ward off and combat disease. NDs view the patient as a complex, interrelated system (a whole person), not as a clogged artery or a tumor. Naturopathic physicians craft comprehensive treatment plans that blend the best of modern medical science and traditional natural medical approaches to not only treat disease, but to also restore health. www.naturopathic.org

Oriental Medicine (also called Traditional Chinese Medicine and Chinese Medicine): Traditional Chinese medicine (TCM) originated in ancient China and has evolved over thousands of years. TCM practitioners use herbs, acupuncture and other methods to treat a wide range of conditions. The TCM view of how the human body works, what causes illness, and how to treat illness is different from Western medicine concepts. www.nccam.nih.gov; www.nccaom.org

Osteopathic Medicine: Developed 130 years ago by A.T. Still, osteopathic medicine is one of the fastest growing healthcare professions in the U.S. and brings a unique philosophy to traditional medicine. With a strong emphasis on the inter-relationship of the body's nerves, muscles, bones and organs, doctors of osteopathic medicine, or DOs, apply the philosophy of treating the whole person to the prevention, diagnosis and treatment of illness, disease and injury. www.osteopathic.org

Patient Protection and Affordable Care Act (PPAC): Federal legislation enacted by Congress in September 2010. Often referred to as "Health Care Reform" and "Obamacare". For details of the Act, implementation dates and FAQ's go to www.healthcare.gov

Planetree: As a global catalyst and leader Planetree promotes the development and implementation of innovative models of healthcare that focus on healing and nurturing body, mind and spirit. Planetree is a non-profit organization that provides education and information in a collaborative community of healthcare organizations, facilitating efforts to create patient centered care in healing environments. www.planetree.org

Physicians for a National Health Plan (PNHP): is a single-issue organization advocating a universal, comprehensive single-payer national health program. PNHP has more than 18,000 members and chapters across the United States. Since 1987, PHNP has advocated for reform in the U.S. health care system. We educate physicians and other health professionals about the benefits of a single-payer system--including fewer administrative costs and affording health insurance for the uninsured. Our members and physician activists work toward a single-payer national health program in their communities. PNHP performs ground breaking research on the health crisis and the need for fundamental reform, coordinates speakers and forums, participates in town hall meetings and debates, contributes scholarly articles to peer-reviewed medical journals, and appears regularly on national television and news programs advocating for a single-payer system. PNHP is the only national physician organization in the United States dedicated exclusively to implementing a single-payer national health program. www.pnhp.org

Portability: The ability to keep a health insurance plan when changing employers.

Preferred Provider Organization (PPO): a type of managed care insurance plan that allows some payment to use a provider who is not in the managed care network, but pays much better for in-network care.

Primary Care Physician (PCP): The physician who is the patient's main contact for all health care needs, and who coordinates all aspects of care with specialists, hospitals, long term care facilities, etc.

Providers: physicians, nurses, hospitals – those people and entities that actually provide health services.

Psychoneuroimmunology: sometimes referred to as PNI. The science of how the nervous system, emotions, and immune system interact and affect one another.

Qi Gong: is the Mandarin Chinese term used to describe various Chinese systems of physical and mental training for health, martial arts and self-enlightenment. Qigong or Chi kung is an English Romanization of two Chinese characters: *Qì* and *Gōng* . The dictionary definition for the word "qi" usually involved the meaning of "breathing", "air", "gas" and "vapor" but it can also be used in the context of describing the relationship between matter, energy and spirit. The dictionary definition for the word "Gong" (功) is that of achievement or results. The two words are combined to describe systems and methods of "energy cultivation" and the manipulation of intrinsic energy within living organisms.

Reiki: Reiki is a healing practice that originated in Japan. Reiki practitioners place their hands lightly on or just above the person receiving treatment, with the goal of facilitating the person's own healing response. People use Reiki to promote overall health and well-being. Reiki is also used by people who are seeking relief from disease-related symptoms and the side effects of conventional medical treatments. Reiki has historically been practiced as a form of self-care. Increasingly, it is also provided by health care professionals in a variety of clinical settings. People do not need a special background to learn how to perform Reiki. Currently, training and certification for Reiki practitioners are not formally regulated. Scientific research is under way to learn more about how Reiki may work, its possible effects on health, and diseases and conditions for which it may be helpful. www.nccam.nih.gov/health/reiki

Risk Pool: is a term used to describe the pooling of similar risks that underlies the concept of insurance. For example, if only one person buys car insurance, the company offering the insurance takes a big risk if that one person has an expensive accident. When thousands of people are insured and pay premiums, the insurance company is counting on very few of them having a claim, and therefore the insurance company stays solvent. When a variety of insureds who have different risks are pooled, the potential for any one of them to have a high insurance claim is lessened. With respect to health insurance, the larger the pool of people covered, and/or the less disease they have, the less likely the insurance company will lose money.

Sastun: The name of the healing amulet Mayan traditional healers use to give them healing energy. Also the name of Dr. Murray's integrative medicine center in Overland Park Kansas. www.sastuncenter.com

Subtle Energy Therapy: see "Energy Healing"

T'ai Chi: **Tai chi chuan** (literal translation "Supreme Ultimate Fist") is an internal Chinese martial art practiced for both its defense training and its health benefits. It is also typically practiced for a variety of other personal reasons: its hard and soft martial arts techniques demonstration competitions, and longevity. As a consequence, a multitude of training forms exist, both traditional and modern, which correspond to those aims. Some of tai chi chuan's training forms are especially known for being practiced at what most people categorize as slow movement.

Therapeutic Touch: Therapeutic Touch (TT) is a technique in which the hands are used to direct human energy for healing purposes. There is usually no actual physical contact. Available scientific evidence does not support many of the claims made for TT, or that energy is balanced or transferred by the use of TT. However, it may be useful in reducing anxiety and increasing the sense of well being in some people. The practice of Therapeutic Touch is based on the belief that problems in the patient's energy field that cause illness and pain can be identified and rebalanced by a healer. Harmful energy is believed to cause blockages and other problems in the patient's normal energy flow, and proponents of TT claim the treatment removes those blockages. TT is promoted by some to improve conditions such as pain, fever, swelling, infections, wounds, ulcers, thyroid problems, colic, burns, nausea, premenstrual syndrome, diarrhea, and headaches. They also say that TT is useful in treating diseases such as measles, Alzheimer's disease, AIDS, asthma, autism, multiple sclerosis, stroke, comas, and cancer. In practice, TT is generally promoted as a complementary therapy, to be used with standard medical care. www.cancer.org; www.therapeutictouch.org

Wholistic Medicine (see Holistic Medicine)

World Health Organization: WHO is the directing and coordinating authority for health within the United Nations system. It is responsible for providing leadership on global health matters, shaping the health research agenda, setting norms and standards, articulating evidence-based policy options, providing technical support to countries and monitoring and assessing health trends. www.who.int

Yoga: The various styles of **yoga** used for health purposes typically combine physical postures, breathing techniques, and meditation or relaxation. People use yoga as part of a general health regimen, and also for a variety of health conditions. www.nccam.nih.gov

APPENDIX

TOOLKIT FOR BEING THE CHANGE

1. **Stress self-assessment tool** – Questions to ask oneself when experiencing stress/ burnout/fatigue and dissatisfaction with one's life

2. **Holmes-Rahe Life Change Stress Scale** – assigns points to stressful life events and correlates the risk of health problems/illness with higher points due to stress

3. **Medical Symptom Questionnaire** – used for adults to assess the severity of health issues; used with permission from The Institute for Functional Medicine, Gig Harbor, WA

4. **Diet Assessment Questionnaire** – a tool used to assess one's intake of healthy and unhealthy nutrients in the diet; used with permission from the Institute for Functional Medicine, Gig Harbor, WA

5. **Working With a Functional Medicine Practitioner** – an outline of what to expect when working with a functional medicine practitioner; used with permission from the Institute for Functional Medicine, Gig Harbor, WA

6. **Exercise/activity log** – a tool to track daily
exercise/activity; used with permission from the
Institute for Functional Medicine, Gig Harbor, WA

7. **Additional resources** for self-care

STRESS SELF-ASSESSMENT TOOL

Am I experiencing a difficult time in my life due to:

1. Too much being demanded of me?
2. I cannot say 'no' when I should?
3. I am not sufficiently in control?
4. I am not sleeping well enough to be rested and stay healthy?
5. I am not keeping fit enough to stay well?
6. I am not living a balanced life?
7. I feel I am infallible, indispensable, indestructible, immortal?
8. I am operating in conflict with my values?

Watkins A, Jonas WB. Mind-Body Medicine: a Clinician's Guide to Psychoneuroimmunology, page 56.

Adult Life Change Scale

Life event	Life change units
Death of a spouse	100
Divorce	73
Marital separation	65
Imprisonment	63
Death of a close family member	63
Personal injury or illness	53
Marriage	50
Dismissal from work	47
Marital reconciliation	45
Retirement	45
Change in health of family member	44
Pregnancy	40
Sexual difficulties	39
Gain a new family member	39
Business readjustment	39
Change in financial state	38
Death of a close friend	37
Change to different line of work	36
Change in frequency of arguments	35
Major mortgage	32
Foreclosure of mortgage or loan	30
Change in responsibilities at work	29
Child leaving home	29
Trouble with in-laws	29

Outstanding personal achievement	28
Spouse starts or stops work	26
Begin or end school	26
Change in living conditions	25
Revision of personal habits	24
Trouble with boss	23
Change in working hours or conditions	20
Change in residence	20
Change in schools	20
Change in recreation	19
Change in church activities	19
Change in social activities	18
Minor mortgage or loan	17
Change in sleeping habits	16
Change in number of family reunions	15
Change in eating habits	15
Vacation	13
Christmas	12
Minor violation of law	11

Score of 300+: At risk of illness.

Score of 150-299+: Risk of illness is moderate (reduced by 30% from the above risk).

Score 150-: Only have a slight risk of illness.

Holmes TH, Rahe RH (1967). "The Social Readjustment Rating Scale". *J Psychosom Res* **11** (2): 213–8

Medical Symptoms Questionnaire

Name _____**Date** _____

Rate each of the following symptoms based upon your typical health
profile for:

Past 30 days   *Past 48 hours*

Point Scale   0 - *Never* or *almost never* have the symptom

                   1 - *Occasionally* have it, effect is *not severe*

                   2 - *Occasionally* have it, effect is *severe*

                   3 - *Frequently* have it, effect is *not severe*

                   4 - *Frequently* have it, effect is *severe*

HEAD   _____   Headaches

               _____   Faintness

               _____   Dizziness

               _____   Insomnia

        Total _____

EYES   _____   Watery or itchy eyes

                  Swollen, reddened or sticky eyelids

_____

               _____   Bags or dark circles under eyes

               _____   Blurred or tunnel vision

(does not include near or far-sightedness)

        Total _____

EARS

      _____ Itchy ears

      _____ Earaches, ear infections

      _____ Drainage from ear

      _____ Ringing in ears, hearing loss

Total _____

NOSE

      _____ Stuffy nose

      _____ Sinus problems

      _____ Hay fever

      _____ Sneezing attacks

      _____ Excessive mucus formation

Total _____

MOUTH/THROAT

      _____Chronic coughing

_____ Gagging, frequent need to clear throat

_____ Sore throat, hoarseness, loss of voice

_____ Swollen or discolored tongue, gums, lips

      _____ Canker sores

Total _____

SKIN

      _____ Acne

      _____ Hives, rashes, dry skin

      _____ Hair loss

      _____ Flushing, hot flashes

      _____ Excessive sweating

Total _____

HEART
        _____ Irregular or skipped heartbeat

        _____ Rapid or pounding heartbeat

        _____ Chest pain

    Total _____

LUNGS
        _____ Chest congestion

        _____ Asthma, bronchitis

        _____ Shortness of breath

        _____ Difficulty breathing

    Total _____

DIGESTIVE TRACT

        _____Nausea, vomiting

        _____ Diarrhea

        _____ Constipation

        _____ Bloated feeling

        _____ Belching, passing gas

        _____ Heartburn

        _____ Intestinal/stomach pain

    Total _____

JOINTS/MUSCLE

        _____ Pain or aches in joints

        _____ Arthritis

_____ Stiffness or limitation of movement

        _____ Pain or aches in muscles

        _____ Feeling of weakness or tiredness

    Total _____

WEIGHT

_____ Binge eating/drinking

_____ Craving certain foods

_____ Excessive weight

_____ Compulsive eating

_____ Water retention

_____ Underweight

Total _____

ENERGY/ACTIVITY

_____ Fatigue, sluggishness

_____ Apathy, lethargy

_____ Hyperactivity

_____ Restlessness

Total _____

MIND

_____ Poor memory

_____ Confusion, poor comprehension

_____ Poor concentration

_____ Poor physical coordination

_____ Difficulty in making decisions

_____ Stuttering or stammering

_____ Slurred speech

_____ Learning disabilities

Total _____

EMOTIONS

_____ Mood swings

_____ Anxiety, fear, nervousness

_____ Anger, irritability, aggressiveness

_____ Depression

Total _____

OTHER   _____   Frequent illness

                 _____   Frequent or urgent urination

                 _____   Genital itch or discharge

        Total _____

GRAND TOTAL   *TOTAL* _____

How Healthy Is Your Diet?

Circle your answers after careful thought, then add up your points (numbers in parentheses).

1. **How many fruits do you *normally* eat each day (1/2 cup fresh or dried fruit, 1 medium piece, 1 cup *unsweetened* juice)?**
   A. 0 (-2)
   B. 1 (0)
   C. 2 to 3 (+2)
   D. 4 or more (+3)

   (score) _____

2. **How many vegetable servings do you *normally* eat each day (1 cup leafy greens, 1/2 cup any other veggie, raw or cooked)?**
   A. 0 (-4)
   B. 1 (0)
   C. 2 (+1)
   D. 3 (+2)
   E. 4 or more (+3)

   (score) _____

3. **How many different varieties of vegetables do you eat in a normal month?**
   A. 2 or less (-4)
   B. 3 to 4 (0)
   C. 5 to 6 (+1)
   D. 7 to 8 (+3)
   E. 9 or more (+4)

   (score) _____

4. How many times do you eat dried beans or peas (legumes, lentils, chickpeas, kidney beans, green peas, etc.) in a normal week?

A. 0 (-2)
B. 1 to 2 (0)
C. 3 to 4 (+1)
D. 5 to 6 (+2)
E. 7 or more (+3)
     (score) _____

5.   How many times do you eat red meat in a normal week?

A. 6 or more (-4)
B. 4 to 5 (-3)
C. 1 to 3 (-1)
D. Less than once a week (+2)
E. 0 (+3)
     (score) _____

6.   How many times do you eat in a fast food restaurant in a normal week?

A. 6 or more (-5)
B. 4 to 5 (-4)
C. 1 to 3 (-3)
D. Less than once a week (-2)
E. 0 (0)
     (score) _____

7.   In a typical day, what do you drink *most* often?
A. Soda (regular or diet) (-4)
B. Caffeinated coffee or tea (-1)
C. Decaffeinated coffee or tea (0)
D. Milk or fruit juice (0)
E. Herbal tea or water (+3)
     (score) _____

8. How many 12 oz. cans of soda do you drink in a normal day?

A. 6 or more (-5)
B. 4 to 5 (-4)
C. 2 to 3 (-3)
D. 1 (-2)
E. Less than 1 (-1)
F. 0 (0)
     (score) _____

9. How often do you eat fish in a typical week?

A. Never (-2)
B. Once (+1)
C. Twice (+2)
D. 3 to 5 times (+3)
     (score) _____

10. In a typical week, how often do you eat whole grains (100% whole grain bread, whole oats, brown rice, quinoa, whole rye crackers)?

A. Never (-3)
B. 1 to 2 times a week (-1)
C. 3 to 4 times a week (0)
D. 5 to 6 times a week (+1)
E. 1 or more times a day (+3)
     (score) _____

11. How often do you eat sweets such as cookies, cakes, or ice cream?

A. 1 or more times a day (-3)
B. Every other day (-2)
C. Twice a week (-1)
D. Once a week (0)
E. 2 to 3 times a month (+1)
F. Rarely (+3)
     (score) _____

Your Total Score_____

Scoring: **22–28** – Great eating habits

               17–21 – Pretty good eating habits

               10–16 – Needs some improvement

               9 or less – Needs much improvement; try to change one habit at a time

Working with a Functional Medicine Practitioner

Functional medicine practitioners promote wellness by focusing on the fundamental underlying factors that influence every patient's experience of health and disease.

The Institute for Functional Medicine teaches practitioners how to assess the patient's fundamental clinical imbalances through careful history taking, physical examination, and laboratory testing. The functional medicine practitioner will consider multiple factors, including:

- **Environmental inputs** – The air you breathe and the water you drink, the particular diet you eat, the quality of the food available to you, your level of physical exercise, and toxic exposures or traumas you have experienced all affect your health.

- **Mind-body connections** – Psychological, spiritual, and social factors all can have a profound influence on your health. Considering these areas helps the functional medicine practitioner see your health in the context of you as a whole person, not just your physical symptoms.

- **Genetic makeup** – Although individual genes may make you more susceptible to some diseases, your DNA is not an unchanging blueprint for your life. Emerging research shows that your genes may be influenced by everything in your environment, as well as your experiences, attitudes, and beliefs. That means it is possible to change the way genes are activated and expressed.

Through assessment of these underlying causes and triggers of dysfunction, the functional medicine practitioner is able to understand how key processes are affected. These are the body's processes that keep you alive. Some occur at the cellular level and involve how cells function, repair, and maintain themselves. These processes are related to larger functions, such as:

The Functional Medicine Approach to Assessment

-how your body rids itself of toxins

-regulation of hormones and neurotransmitters

-immune system function

-inflammatory responses

-digestion and absorption of nutrients and the health of the digestive tract

-structural integrity

-psychological and spiritual equilibrium

-how you produce energy

All of these processes are influenced by both environmental factors and your genetic make-up; when they are disturbed or imbalanced, they lead to symptoms, which can lead to disease if effective interventions are not applied.

Most imbalances in functionality can be addressed; some can be completely restored to optimum function, and others can be substantially improved.

- **Prevention is paramount.** Virtually every complex, chronic disease is preceded by long-term disturbances in functionality that can be identified and effectively managed.

- **Changing how the systems function can have a major impact on the patient's health.** The functional medicine practitioner examines a wide array of available interventions and customizes a treatment plan including those with the most impact on underlying functionality.

- **Functional medicine expands the clinician's tool kit.** Treatments may include combinations of drugs, botanical medicines, nutritional supplements, therapeutic diets, or detoxification programs. They may also include counseling on lifestyle, exercise, or stress-management techniques.

- **The patient becomes a partner.** As a patient, you become an active partner with your functional medicine practitioner. This allows you to really be in charge of improving your own health and changing the outcome of disease.

The Institute for Functional Medicine is a nonprofit educational organization

Visit us at **www.functionalmedicine.org** or call us at **1-800-228-0622**

Exercise/Aerobic Conditioning Log

Name: _____ Date: _____

Target Heart Rate = 220 – _____ (age) × _____(0.5, 0.6, 0.8)

Beats/minute_____   Beats/10 seconds _____

	Mon	Tue	Wed	Thu	Fri	Sat	Sun
Week 1: type of exercise							
Time of day/ length of exercise							
Resting heart rate							
Aerobic heart rate							
Comments							
Week 2: type of exercise							
Time of day/ length of exercise							
Resting heart rate							
Aerobic heart rate							

Comments							
Week 3: type of exercise							
Time of day/ length of exercise							
Resting heart rate							
Aerobic heart rate							
Comments							
	Mon	**Tue**	**Wed**	**Thu**	**Fri**	**Sat**	**Sun**
Week 4: type of exercise							
Time of day/ length of exercise							
Resting heart rate							
Aerobic heart rate							
Comments							
Week 5: type of exercise							
Time of day/ length of exercise							

Resting heart rate							
Aerobic heart rate							
Comments							
Week 6: type of exercise							
Time of day/ length of exercise							
Resting heart rate							
Aerobic heart rate							
Comments							

ADDITIONAL RESOURCES FOR SELF CARE

"Healthcare Treatment Directives" and "Durable Power of Attorney for Health Care Decisions" as well as assistance with conducting discussions about end of life decisions for patients, family members and health professionals available from the **Center for Practical Bioethics** at 816-221-1100 and www.practicalbioethics.org

National Council on Alcoholism and Drug Dependence – self-assessment tools for helping determine of one has a substance problem and resources for help. www.recovery.org

TO ORDER ADDITIONAL COPIES:

www.rainydaybooks.com

www.amazon.com

www.lulu.com

For more information or to offer comments:

Sastun Center of Integrative Medicine

10875 Grandview

Overland Park, Kansas 66210

Tel: (913) 345-0060

Fax: (913) 345-0090

www.sastuncenter.com

info@sastuncenter.com

www.ingramcontent.com/pod-product-compliance
Lightning Source LLC
Chambersburg PA
CBHW071414170526
45165CB00001B/271